BARRON'S BOOK NOTES

JONATHAN SWIFT'S
Gulliver's Travels

BY
Marguerite Feitlowitz

SERIES EDITOR
Michael Spring
Editor, *Literary Cavalcade*
Scholastic Inc.

BARRON'S

BARRON'S EDUCATIONAL SERIES, INC.
Woodbury, New York / London / Toronto / Sydney

ACKNOWLEDGMENTS

We would like to acknowledge the many painstaking hours of work
Holly Hughes and Thomas F. Hirsch have devoted to making the
Book Notes series a success.

All inquiries should be addressed to:
Barron's Educational Series, Inc.
113 Crossways Park Drive
Woodbury, New York 11797

Library of Congress Catalog Card No. 84-18501

International Standard Book No. 0-8120-3416-3

Library of Congress Cataloging in Publication Data
Feitlowitz, Marguerite.
    Jonathan Swift's Gulliver's travels.

    (Barron's book notes)
    Bibliography: p. 100
    Summary: A guide to reading "Gulliver's Travels"
with a critical and appreciative mind. Includes
background on the author's life and times, sample
tests, term paper suggestions, and a reading list.
    1. Swift, Jonathan, 1667–1745. Gulliver's travels.
[1. Swift, Jonathan, 1667–1745. Gulliver's travels.
2. English literature—History and criticism] I. Title.
PR3724.G8F4   1984   823'.5   84-18501
ISBN 0-8120-3416-3 (pbk.)

PRINTED IN THE UNITED STATES OF AMERICA

456   550   98765432

CONTENTS

ADVISORY BOARD

HOW TO USE THIS BOOK

You have to know how to approach literature in order to get the most out of it. This *Barron's Book Notes* volume follows a plan based on methods used by some of the best students to read a work of literature.

Begin with the guide's section on the author's life and times. As you read, try to form a clear picture of the author's personality, circumstances, and motives for writing the work. This background usually will make it easier for you to hear the author's tone of voice, and follow where the author is heading.

Then go over the rest of the introductory material—such sections as those on the plot, characters, setting, themes, and style of the work. Underline, or write down in your notebook, particular things to watch for, such as contrasts between characters and repeated literary devices. At this point, you may want to develop a system of symbols to use in marking your text as you read. (Of course, you should only mark up a book you own, not one that belongs to another person or a school.) Perhaps you will want to use a different letter for each character's name, a different number for each major theme of the book, a different color for each important symbol or literary device. Be prepared to mark up the pages of your book as you read. Put your marks in the margins so you can find them again easily.

Now comes the moment you've been waiting for—the time to start reading the work of literature. You may want to put aside your *Barron's Book Notes* volume until you've read the work all the way through. Or you may want to alternate, reading the *Book Notes* analysis of each section as soon as you have finished reading the corresponding part of the original. Before you move on, reread crucial passages you don't fully understand. (Don't take this guide's analysis for granted—make up your own mind as to what the work means.)

Once you've finished the whole work of literature, you may want to review it right away, so you can firm up your ideas about what it means. You may want to leaf through the book concentrating on passages you marked in reference to one character or one theme. This is also a good time to reread the *Book Notes* introductory material, which pulls together insights on specific topics.

When it comes time to prepare for a test or to write a paper, you'll already have formed ideas about the work. You'll be able to go back through it, refreshing your memory as to the author's exact words and perspective, so that you can support your opinions with evidence drawn straight from the work. Patterns will emerge, and ideas will fall into place; your essay question or term paper will almost write itself. Give yourself a dry run with one of the sample tests in the guide. These tests present both multiple-choice and essay questions. An accompanying section gives answers to the multiple-choice questions as well as suggestions for writing the essays. If you have to select a term paper topic, you may choose one from the list of suggestions in this book. This guide also provides you with a reading list, to help you when you start research for a term paper, and a selection of provocative comments by critics, to spark your thinking before you write.

THE AUTHOR AND HIS TIMES

Gulliver's Travels was an overnight success, a runaway bestseller. And why not? Not only did it smack of mystery and political, social, and sexual scandal, but it's often hilarious, and just about always brilliant.

Swift was dean of St. Patrick's Cathedral in Dublin when his novel came out. Since in this book he wrote about—and often harpooned—prominent political figures, he published the book anonymously. While most readers were trying like mad to find out who the author was, Swift's close friends had great fun keeping the secret. Days after the publication of the *Travels*, Alexander Pope, one of Swift's dearest friends and the author of such important works as "The Rape of the Lock" and "An Essay on Man," wrote him in an especially playful letter: "Motte [Swift's publisher] receiv'd the copy (he tells me) he knew not from whence, nor from whom, dropp'd at his house in the dark, from a Hackney-coach: by computing the time, I found it was after you left England, so for my part, I suspend my judgment." Pope, of course, knew perfectly well that Swift was the author of *Gulliver's Travels*.

London fairly buzzed with speculations, suggestions, and countersuggestions regarding the author's identity, as well as those of some of his characters. In Part I, for example, the Lilliputian Emperor—tyrannical, cruel, corrupt, and obsessed with ceremony—though a timeless symbol of bad government, is also a biting satire of George I, King of England (from 1714 to 1727), during much of Swift's career. The Lilliputian Empress stands for Queen Anne, who blocked Swift's advancement in the Church of England, having taken offense at some of his earlier, signed satires. There are two political parties in Lilliput, the Low-Heels and the High-Heels. These correspond respectively to the Whigs and Tories, the two major British political parties.

It didn't take long for people to catch on to the fact that the author was writing about England by way of Lilliput, Bröbdingnag, Laputa, and the land of the Houyhnhnms. And it also didn't take long for the public to discover that the author was Jonathan Swift. Not only had he been involved in some of the most important and heated political events of the time, but he was also a well-known political journalist and satirist whose style was, to say the least, distinctive.

Swift got his political feet wet in the Glorious Revolution (1688–89), the object of which was to convince James II (king of England from 1685 to 1688) to abdicate the throne. James, a Roman Catholic, sought to increase the power of the Roman Church in England at the expense of the Anglican Church, long considered the country's official church. James' interests ran counter to those of the majority of his subjects, which was bad enough, but his methods—underhanded, blatantly discriminatory against Anglicans (also called Episcopalians), and cruel—made the situation impossible. James did flee England in December 11, 1688, when William of Orange, his son-in-law and a moderate Protestant, arrived with a small army to depose him. James lived the rest of his life in France under the protection of Louis XIV, but the English remained anxious that he or his son would again try to seize the throne.

At this point, Swift was secretary to Sir William Temple, a prominent Whig. Though Swift (an Anglican clergyman, remember) welcomed the Protestant William of Orange, he was uneasy that the monarch was so lenient toward Roman Catholics. Swift, for example, favored the Test Act, which required all government officials to take the Sacraments according to the rites of the Anglican Church. This measure, of course, would exclude Catholics and other non-Anglicans from holding government posts. This put Swift at odds with the Whig party which, like the king, favored the repeal of the Test Act. By 1710 it became clear that the Whig government would fall. After making sure that the Tories would favor his policies for a strong Church of England, Swift changed parties.

All of Part I of the *Travels* is an allegorical account of British politics during the turbulent early eighteenth century, when the main political parties, the Tories and the Whigs, competed with each other bitterly. England is a limited monarchy. There is a king and/or queen, whose power is checked by Parliament, especially the House of Commons which consists of representatives of the people. In Swift's time the Tories tended to be a more conservative party: they supported a strong monarchy and a strong Church of England; they were hostile to the new mercantile classes; their support came mostly from the landed gentry and clergy. The Whigs, on the other hand, emphasized the parliamentary aspect of the government, supported the rise of the new middle class, and were more religiously tolerant than the Tories. The Whigs were a more varied group than the Tories, and drew support from the new middle class, sectors of the nobility who hadn't profited from James II's abdication, bankers and financiers, as well as Catholics and other non-Anglican members.

From 1710 to 1714 Swift, who was now a Tory, remember, was one of the most influential members of the English government. As editor of the *Examiner*, the Tory party organ, he was also one of the most famous political journalists of his day. He was very close to Oxford and Bolingbroke, heads of the Tories (they also appear, in various "disguises," in Part I). Swift wrote in support of the Peace of Utrecht (1713), which ended the War of the Spanish Succession with France and Spain. This war is recounted allegorically in Book I as the war between Lilliput (England) and Blefuscu (France).

While in London Swift worked passionately for his political ideals. He expected that in return for his efforts he'd be rewarded with a bishopric in England. That way he would remain close to London, the center of activity. He was slighted, however, and given the deanship of St. Patrick's in Dublin. This was a blow from which many say Swift never really recovered. He felt as though he'd been banished, unfairly, and in many ways he had been.

Despite his disappointment Swift worked hard for his church in Ireland and for the cause of Irish freedom against the Whigs, many of whom considered Ireland more of a colony than a country. For most of the rest of his life, Swift was a clergyman/writer/activist. In 1729, when he was sixty-three, he wrote *A Modest Proposal*, considered by many to be the best satire ever written in English. In it Swift makes use of the persona of a respectable Whig businessman. His protagonist makes the suggestion that the Irish should fatten their children so that they could grace the tables—in the form of food—of the English. This would solve two problems, argued Swift's Whig.

First, it would relieve Ireland's overpopulation problem. Second, English lords wouldn't have to import meat from so far away. In *A Modest Proposal* Swift made his readers take notice of the dire situation in Ireland, *and* he pointed a finger at the English who he considered responsible for it and callous about it, to boot.

Swift's aims in the *Proposal* were humanitarian, yet his satire cut like a knife. This is in keeping with Swift's contradictory personality, which makes him one of the most puzzling figures in English literature. Acknowledged as a brilliant man of his age, he was a poor student. He entered the church reluctantly as a way of earning a living, yet he quickly became an ambitious and influential clergymen. His harsh satires caused many to call him a misanthrope, one who hates people. Yet he was a very outgoing man, a dazzler in the sparkling intellectual/literary/political/social constellation of John Dryden, Alexander Pope, John Gay, John Arbuthnot, Joseph Addison, and Richard Steele. He wrote many letters, and with few exceptions, they are witty, charming, and lively.

Even Swift's biographers have had to live with the hard fact that the story of Swift's life is hidden behind the public events, the verifiable dates, and the published works. For all his activism and close relations with public figures, we know surprisingly little about the private Swift. No one even knows if Swift ever married. He had a years-long, passionate relationship with Esther Johnson and many have suspected that the two were secretly married. Though they saw each other every day, they didn't live together, and always visited in the company of a chaperone. Swift's famous *Journal to Stella*, in which he satirizes his own fame and writing (another contradiction—he worked hard to achieve recognition, and obviously wanted it badly), was written from 1710 to 1714 while he was in London with the Tories. Swift also had an involvement with a woman he called Vanessa (her real name was Hester Vanhomrich), who left England to be with Swift in Ireland. They also didn't live together, though Vanessa was devoted to Swift for years. Because Swift died insane, some biographers have suggested that he never married because he'd contracted syphilis as a young man and feared passing it on. We'll never know.

We do know, however, that Swift was born in Dublin on November 30, 1667. Swift's father, an English lawyer, died while his wife was pregnant with Jonathan. Right after Jonathan was born his mother left him to be raised by her brother. Jonathan, never a good student, was graduated from Trinity College as a favor to his uncle. He worked halfheartedly on a masters degree, but left to join the Glorious Revolution.

From then on we have a pretty full accounting of his public deeds, but the private man remains mysterious. Swift was simultaneously praised to the skies and criticized severely for *Gulliver's Travels*. His admirers called attention to the literary merits of the book and its ultimately humanitarian concerns; his critics said he hated mankind and cited his invention of the Yahoos as proof. It seems impossible to have a lukewarm opinion on Swift; the work is too strong and his personality, as his contemporaries tell it, seemed larger than life. As in the work there are few "mellow" passages, so Swift seemed to swing from one extreme mood to another.

Swift's last years were a torment. He suffered awful bouts of dizziness, nausea, deafness, and mental incapacity. In fact, Swift's harshest critics tried to discredit the *Travels* on the grounds that the author was mad when he wrote it. But he wasn't. The *Travels* were published in 1726—and Part IV, which raised the most controversy, was written before Part III—and Swift didn't enter a mental institution until 1742. He died in 1745.

Gulliver's Travels, which you're about to explore, may well be the world's most brilliant "homework assignment." Along with Pope, Arbuthnot, Gay, and other literary lights, Swift was a member of The Martinus Scriblerus Club. The purpose of this club was to satirize the foolishness of modern man. Each member was given a topic; Swift's was to satirize the current "boom" in travel literature. The final result, ten years later, was *Gulliver's Travels*.

THE NOVEL

The Plot

Gulliver's Travels is the tale of Lemuel Gulliver as he voyages to the strange lands of Lilliput, Brobdingnag, the kingdom of Laputa, and the land of the Houyhnhnms.

In Lilliput people are six inches high, and Gulliver, in comparison, is a giant, or a "Man-Mountain," as they call him. This section of the novel (Part I) is essentially an allegory of English politics in the early eighteenth century when the Whigs and Tories were fighting bitterly for control of the country. Correspondingly, Gulliver becomes involved with the domestic and international dealings of the Lilliputian government. Legislation is drafted and enacted to deal with Gulliver's physical presence and needs; an official document outlining the terms of his freedom is drawn up. One of these terms is that Gulliver must aid the Lilliputians in their war against Blefuscu (Lilliput represents England, Blefuscu, France). Gulliver literally seizes the enemy fleet and strides across the harbor with it back to Lilliput. For a short time he's a hero.

But Gulliver intervenes in the peace process, and wins a more advantageous treaty for the Blefuscudians than they would otherwise have had. After that it's downhill for Gulliver in Lilliput. When he urinates onto a fire raging in the palace and thereby saves the royal chambers, he is impeached for disobeying an ordinance prohibiting public urination. This and some other trumped-up charges against Gulliver result in a conviction of high treason, punishable by blinding. Gulliver escapes to Blefuscu, then home to England.

Part II, which takes place in the land of Brobdingnag, continues the allegory on English politics. This time, however, it's Gulliver—every inch the Lilliputian among the giant Brobdingnagians—who represents English ways. After a short stint as a working freak, Gulliver is rescued by the king and queen and lives a life of considerable comfort at court. He spends much of his time learning the language and talking with the king about life in England. The king emerges as a fair, merciful ruler and a very sympathetic and humane man. Gulliver, in contrast, seems as petty, vindictive, and cruel as the Lilliputians.

One day while on an outing with the king and queen, Gulliver's "box" (his house) is kidnapped by a bird (with him inside), and dropped in the sea, and recovered by an English ship. Gulliver stays in England a while with his family then goes back to sea.

In Part III, where Gulliver goes to the flying island of Laputa and some of its colonies nearby, you get a sort of "allegorical whirlwind tour" of early eighteenth-century scientific activities and attitudes. His first stop is Laputa, where the inhabitants have one eye turned inward and one eye turned up to the sky—they're thinking *always* of their own speculations (inward) and of lofty issues in mathematics, astronomy and music (upward). They're so fixated they need "flappers" to box them on the ear to let them know someone is talking to them. The Laputans are so distracted from everyday life that they're barely conscious of their wives (who fornicate with their lovers right in front of them, knowing they'll never be noticed). Because the Laputans are despotic rulers of their colonies, and because they pay precious little attention to Gulliver, he gets sick of them and goes on to the island of Balnibarbi.

There Gulliver becomes friendly with Count Munodi, who is the only one on the island who lives in a beautiful, well-built house and whose lands yield crops. The others—Projectors, most of them, engaged in "advanced" scientific research—do everything according to the most "sophisticated" theories. Consequently their houses are in ruins and their lands lie fallow. Gulliver visits the Academy of the Projectors to learn more about them, and witnesses a series of perfectly useless, wasteful experiments.

In Glubdubbdrib Gulliver is able to call up historical figures from the past and converse with them.

In Luggnagg Gulliver meets the Struldbruggs, a race of people who live forever. They do not have eternal youth, though; rather, they grow perpetually older, more feeble, miserable, and useless.

Gulliver returns to England before again setting sail.

In Part IV Gulliver, after a mutiny, ends up in the land of the Houyhnhnms (pronounced WHIN-nims). The Houyhnhnms are horses governed totally by reason. They have created a society that is perfectly ordered, perfectly peaceful (except for the Yahoos), and exempt from the topsy-turviness of passion. The Yahoos are humans, but are so bestial that they are human only in outward appearance. The Yahoos are kept in a kennel, and are prohibited from having anything to do with the Houyhnhnms. The Yahoos arrived here by accident.

Gulliver tries his best to become a Houyhnhnm— he talks like them, walks like them, tries to think and act like them. He's in the anxious position of being neither a Yahoo nor a Houyhnhnm; he fits nowhere, and because of this he must leave. Gulliver goes mad in Part IV, and can never reconcile himself to other people, whom he considers Yahoos. Neither can be come to terms with the Yahoo part of himself.

Back in England, he buys horses and spends most of his time in the stable. He can barely tolerate the presence of his family, and has as little to do with them as possible. He says that his aim in writing *Gulliver's Travels* is to correct the Yahoos. Having been exposed to the Houyhnhnms, he feels he is the man for the job.

The Characters

Swift's characters aren't the well-rounded, "flesh and blood" characters you usually find in a skillfully written novel. His characters are allegorical; that is, they stand for something—an idea, an attitude, a posture—or someone else. It's never simple with Swift. Gulliver, for instance, represents different things at different points in the novel. In Part I Gulliver is solid, decent, and responsible. At times in Lilliput (during the inventory sequence in Chapter II for example), Gulliver stands for Lords Oxford and Bolingbroke. In Part II Gulliver represents a man who under repeated attacks on his ego and self-image succumbs to pettiness and vindictiveness characteristic of the Lilliputians.

Swift's allegories are never black and white. Even the Lilliputians have their good points—they *are* very clever. And the Houyhnhnms, who have created a perfectly orderly society in which there are not even words to describe anger, lying, and disagreement, let alone the more serious vices, have their drawbacks, subtle though they may be. A life without passion may always be calm, but is it life as humans know it, and could live it?

Part III may be the exception, in that the Laputans and Projectors do tend to be black and white. Many critics feel that because of this, Swift's satire, from an artistic standpoint, is weaker here than in the other books. You will have to decide this for yourself.

Bear in mind that in *Gulliver's Travels* there's no character you can follow as you can a traditional omniscient narrator. Swift's satire is designed to keep you an independent reader, the characters are meant to stimulate you, not to lead you.

Lemuel Gulliver

Gulliver is the most important character in this novel. He's the "author" of the *Travels*, he's your tour guide. He's also one of the most vexing characters in English literature.

Gulliver's frustrating to deal with for a number of reasons. 1. He's not steady; he changes in relation to the places he visits and the events that befall him as he voyages. 2. He's often a victim of Swift's satire. This means that we have to be on our guard against what he says, and even though he's our guide, we can't follow him everywhere. If we do, he'll lead us into madness. 3. It's impossible to feel relaxed with Gulliver, as we can with a traditional omniscient narrator. Swift won't let us trust him enough for that. 4. Because Gulliver directs a lot of his hostility toward us—readers beyond reform—we in turn feel hostile toward him. 5. Looking at Gulliver is a lot like looking in a mirror. We are by turns fascinated, attracted, disgusted, and ashamed.

You first meet Gulliver at the "end" of his story, in a letter he's written to his publisher. By now Gulliver is out of his mind: he's raving, he's nasty, he lies, he's proud beyond the limits of pride. But he wasn't always.

He grew up in Nottinghamshire, the third of five sons in a respectable, middle-class family. While in school he held jobs: as an apprentice, he proved his competence; as a physician, he was able to get work on ships, which had been his lifelong dream. Before Gulliver leaves for Lilliput it can be said that he's reasonably intelligent, hard working, disciplined, alert, and curious. As a traveler in Lilliput he's careful in his observations, complete in his descriptions. Occupied as he is with the surface of things, he's a bit naïve. Gulliver is a good, all-around type of guy.

But he gets knocked around while he's traveling, and this affects his character. In Lilliput he seems to be eminently fair-minded compared to the cunning, vindictive, petty Lilliputians. Literally a giant in their land, Gulliver never takes unfair advantage of his size in his dealing with them. Though they're violent with him, he never retaliates in kind.

In Brobdingnag, land of the giants, Gulliver appears Lilliputian in more ways than one. But his size is a dire problem to him here. He is frequently injured, the king's dwarf takes out his frustrations on tiny Gulliver, but the latter is an improvement for Gulliver—before coming to court, his master hired him out as a freak at village fairs. Gulliver can't keep it together under the strain of repeated attacks on his ego, and in his dealings with the Brobdingnagian king, Gulliver appears as nasty and cruel as the Lilliputians themselves.

Gulliver recedes in Part III. Not much happens to him *personally*, for the most part he recounts what he observes in the way of scientific experiments. Swift uses Gulliver to relate deadpan what he himself considers to be foolish attitudes and activities.

Gulliver goes mad in Part IV. Presented with the Houyhnhnms and the Yahoos, Gulliver tries desperately to become a Houyhnhnm, an animal governed entirely by reason. He cannot, of course. Gulliver isn't able to see the Yahoos as Swift intends them to be seen—as representing the worst traits in human nature, and the lowest level to which he might sink. Gulliver sees the Yahoos as mankind, period. Gulliver also misapprehends the Houyhnhnms. It is only to Gulliver—not to Swift—that these creatures represent a human ideal. Gulliver, neither Yahoo nor Houyhnhnm, can find no species to which he belongs, and so goes mad.

When the *Travels* first came out Swift was attacked for misanthropy, largely on the basis of Gulliver's hostility to humans in Part IV. Highly influential critics, such as William Thackeray (whose novels include *Vanity Fair* and *Henry Esmond, Esq.*) equated Gulliver with Swift. This is a misreading of the book, but the notion remains an important part of the early history of critical reaction to *Gulliver's Travels*. You must come to terms with Gulliver and with the uses Swift has for Gulliver. Be alert for the instances when Swift and Gulliver overlap, when Gulliver says something with which Swift agrees; for the instances when Swift lets us know that Gulliver's viewpoint is one among many; and for the instances when Swift holds Gulliver up for our criticism.

The Lilliputian Emperor

On one level, the Lilliputian emperor represents George I of England. Swift had no admiration for this king, and uses Lilliputian court practices allegorically to criticize the English monarch. On another level the tiny emperor represents tyranny, cruelty, lust for power, and corruption. He is a timeless symbol of bad government.

Flimnap

This is a Lilliputian government official who represents Robert Walpole, the Whig prime minister under George I. Walpole was Swift's enemy.

The Lilliputian Empress

The empress represents Queen Anne, who blocked Swift's advancement in the Church of England because she was offended by his writings. The empress bears early responsibility for Gulliver's demise in Lilliput.

The Lilliputians in general

The Lilliputians are tiny creatures, possessed of ingenuity, craft, and cunning. They have a love of flourish, pomp, ceremony, and bureaucracy. They appreciate military parades, theatrical oratory, and political maneuverings of any kind, including gossip. They are very refined in their manners, but this doesn't prevent them from being petty, vindictive, and vengeful.

The Brobdingnagian Farmer

He is a poor man who seizes on Gulliver as a way to earn money. Like many who have suffered and who suddenly see an end to their poverty, he's unable to care about the suffering he's imposing on Gulliver.

The Brobdingnagian King

This man represents Swift's idea of a just, wise, and strong ruler. For him, force is a measure of absolute last resort, and the notion of gunpowder (of which he'd never heard until Gulliver described it to him) horrifies him. The king has other admirable traits—he's curious, eager to learn, not afraid of the unknown. He spends long hours with Gulliver asking him questions about English and European domestic and public ways, politics, religion, and history.

Glumdalclitch

Glumdalclitch is the daughter of the Brobdingnagian farmer. She is Gulliver's nursemaid and loves him and cares for him as her dearest doll.

The Brobdingnagian Queen

She, too, regards Gulliver as a pet. Yet it was she who rescued Gulliver from the farmer and convinced her husband that they adopt him. She is kind, though she sometimes embarrasses Gulliver by treating him like a baby, or a prized puppy.

The Brobdingnagians in general

The Brobdingnagians in general are as ugly to Gulliver as the Lilliputians were physically attractive. Though their appetites appear bestially large to Gulliver, their features grotesque, and their skin revolting, the Brobdingnagian character is much more refined compared to the Lilliputian.

The Laputans

These creatures have one eye turned inward and one turned up to the sky to indicate that they are so absorbed in their abstract speculations that they can't see what's going on around them. They represent science cut off from the demands of real life, and reason so abstract it is folly.

The Projectors

These are Swift's allegorical treatment of certain members of England's Royal Society, scientists and scholars engaged in experimentation intended to yield practical applications. Their projects, modeled on actual Royal Society experiments done in Swift's time, are nonsensical and wasteful. The Projectors have no regard for tradition; they are concerned only with what's new.

Count Munodi

Count Munodi lives in Lagado, land of the Projectors. Unlike them, however, he has great respect for wise traditions of the past. Accordingly, his house is built on fine architectural principles and solid traditional construction. His land is fertile, as he cultivates it the way lands have been worked for centuries. He is despised for being out of step with the times. Many readers think Count Munodi represents Lords Oxford and/or Bolingbroke, also considered out of step by the Whigs, who wholeheartedly embraced the Enlightenment.

The Struldbruggs

These creatures, whom Gulliver encounters in Part III, live forever. They are, however, far from the stereotypical fantasy figures who have eternal youth and vitality. The Struldbruggs keep getting older and are probably the most miserable beings alive.

The Houyhnhnms

These horses are governed entirely by reason. They have created a society in which there is no crime, no poverty, no disagreement, no unhappiness. Neither is there any joy, passion, ecstatic love. Everything is always on an even keel. Husbands and wives (marriages are arranged according to gene pools) have no more feeling for each other than for anyone else. More than anything, Gulliver wants to be a Houyhnhnm. To him, these creatures represent the human ideal. To Swift, the Houyhnhnms represent what life would be like without the passionate "spice" that makes it worth living. Still, their society is admirable in certain regards. Do you think you could live among the Houyhnhnms? Would you want to be one?

The Yahoos

The Yahoos are so startling and unforgettable that the term has stayed in our language. When someone today refers to a person as a Yahoo, he means that that person is a hick, somewhat less than civilized. To Swift, it meant something for more damning.

The Yahoos in *Gulliver's Travels* embody the lowest traits in human nature. They are gluttonous, filthy, lascivious, thieving, violent brutes. Only physically do they resemble civilized people. They live in kennels and function as the Houyhnhnms' "horses."

To Gulliver they represent mankind, period. To Swift, they represent what man must strive to overcome. Bear in mind that the Yahoos ended up on the Houyhnhnms' island by accident. A female and a male arrived, and, stranded, never left. The original couple had children, so did their children, etc. Totally cut off from other humans, they degenerated to the level of beasts. It's possible that Swift is saying here that people need to be with other people to remain civilized. Swift, who has been attacked for misanthropy, is actually arguing *against* it here.

Captain Pedro de Mendez

Pedro de Mendez is the captain of the ship that rescues Gulliver when the Houyhnhnms send him away. Mendez is the first person Gulliver has seen in two years. He is extremely gentle, generous, and patient with Gulliver. Not only does he take Gulliver back to Europe, he makes sure he gets special food, clothing, and quarters. He is immediately sensitive to the fact that Gulliver is traumatized, and he suffers Gulliver's insults without batting an eyelash. He convinces Gulliver to go home to his family, and pays his way from Amsterdam to England.

Swift's creation of the character Pedro de Mendez is a good indication that he never intended the Yahoos to represent his estimation of mankind.

Other Elements

SETTING

Written in the form of a travel book, *Gulliver's Travels* has a variety of settings, each of which symbolizes one or more of Swift's themes. Gulliver stands out in relief against these settings; each brings out different parts of his personality. We get to know Gulliver, and Gulliver gets to know himself, through comparison and contrast to those around him. Because the settings change, and Gulliver finds himself in contrasting situations, Gulliver's viewpoints (as well as our own) are constantly shifting.

Part I takes place in Lilliput, where the inhabitants are six inches high, and Gulliver seems a giant. Swift makes his question literal: What is it to be small? What are the many forms of smallness? What is the value of doing things on a small scale? The hazards? Over the years many critics have suggested that in Part I Gulliver is looking down the Great Chain of Being at the Lilliputians who are petty, cruel, benighted. In comparison, Gulliver's (man's) place on the chain seems secure, somewhere between animals and angels. Yet this is Swift, so things don't remain so simple. The Lilliputians have the refinement (to Gulliver), the physical attractiveness, and ingenuity we normally associate with human beings. Gulliver's bulk renders him more animallike, in that he is a *physical* problem in Lilliput. Bestial as he seems at times, Gulliver is the humanitarian.

The Lilliputians represent the Whigs for whom Swift has so much contempt. Their political ways correspond to Whig machinations in English government in the early eighteenth century.

Part II takes place in Brobdingnag, the land of giants. What does it mean to be big? What are the forms of bigness? The values of it? The hazards in it? Here Gulliver has been said to be looking up the Great Chain of Being—he may seem physically very refined here, but he's no humanitarian. The Brobdingnagians represent what Swift considers good rulers and politicians.

Part III constitutes a "whirlwind tour" of Enlightenment intellectual and scientific attitudes and practices.

In Part IV, the world is stood on its head—animals rule and people are kept in cages.

THEMES

The overarching theme of this novel is the question, 'What is it to be human?' You follow Gulliver through four traumatic voyages, you are exposed to a host of creatures and situations and systems of their devising that help you to form an answer to this question.

But let's break it down.

1. HUMAN NATURE IS PETTY
The Lilliputians and Gulliver among the Brobdingnagians make a good case for the pettiness of human nature.

2. HUMAN NATURE IS MAGNANIMOUS AND JUST
The Brobdingnagians and Pedro de Mendez are fine examples of generosity and fairness.

3. MAN IS SOMEWHERE BETWEEN PETTINESS AND MAGNANIMITY
There are two ways of looking at this theme: either man is capable of improving himself, or he is not. Bear in mind that Swift was a traditional cleric who held

the view that man's task on earth is to better himself spiritually, to get as far as possible from the Yahoo parts of his character. On the other hand, the Yahoos make an extremely strong impression and Gulliver never fully recovers from his exposure to them. It seems it's an individual thing—some people can and some can't.

4. THE SIN OF PRIDE IS THE MOST DANGEROUS SIN OF ALL

Gulliver at the end is guilty of pride even as he inveighs against it. He is most like a Yahoo at this moment. Trace the attacks against Gulliver's pride throughout the four books, and the fatal blows to his ego.

5. WHAT IS GOOD GOVERNMENT?

Contrast the governments of Lilliput and Brobdingnag.

6. WHAT IS THE PROPER PLACE AND USE OF SCIENCE AND THE ABSTRACT DISCIPLINES?

Consider the follies committed in Part III.

7. WHAT IS THE VALUE OF TRADITION?

Consider the contempt for tradition among the Projectors in Part III.

8. WHAT IS THE FUNCTION OF RELIGION?

Is it a means to attain political power, as in Lilliput? Are religious differences really worth going to war over? Is religion a means whereby man might improve himself spiritually?

9. WHAT ARE THE VALUES OF REASON?

Consider not only the most sensible aspects of Houyhnhnm society, but Lilliputian ingenuity, Brobdingnagian justice and forebearance, and the kindness and patience of Pedro de Mendez.

10. WHAT ARE THE LIMITS OF REASON?

Think of the dryness of many Houyhnhnm ways. Think, too, of the ways in which Lilliputians and Laputans distort reason and its powers.

Notice that many of these themes contradict each other. Swift was writing to vex you, to startle you into deep reflection, to invite debate.

STYLE

Swift's style is composed chiefly of *satire*, *allegory*, and *irony*. Satire consists of a mocking attack against vices, stupidities, and follies, with an aim to educate, edify, improve. Allegory is one of Swift's most important satirical tools. Allegory is a device in which characters, situations, and places have a significance that goes beyond simply what they are in themselves. Allegory, like satire, is used to teach. The Lilliputians, for example, are allegorical Whigs. The Academy of Projectors is an allegory of the Royal Society. In order to make his devastating case against the Whigs, for example, Swift needs the disguise (the allegory) of the Lilliputians. He could never have actually named real names in his novel. The Yahoos are an allegory for a part of man's nature. Notice how important a part *exaggeration* plays in Swiftian allegory.

Irony is when the intended meaning of a statement or an action is opposite to that which is presented. A fine example of Swiftian irony is when Gulliver says he saw no mercy in the Lilliputian decision to blind him. Gulliver was actually looking for the mercy here, and, of course, there was none to be found. It is also ironic that the Brobdingnagians appear gross, but are filled with beauty.

Swiftian satire is a complicated affair. You've seen how even when he's using Gulliver to satirize the Lilliputians, for example, Swift is satirizing Gulliver. And then Swift satirizes the reader by creating a great tension between what is and what appears to be. He seems always to be prodding us, "What do you *really* think, beneath your nice appearance, polite ways, and evidence of intelligence?" It's hard not to fall into Swift's trap. The most obvious Swiftian trap, of course, is Gulliver himself, your tour guide—an affable, respectable, conscientious man. But if you follow him all the way, he'll lead you to madness.

Swift also satirizes himself through Gulliver. Gulliver ranting that mankind is beyond improvement is Swift flagellating himself for even trying. Yet, of course, there's tension here, too, for Swift has written the book. The tension within Swift is communicated directly to us, for if he fails as a satirist, it's because we've failed as human beings. But Swift satirizes because overridingly he cares, and thinks we, and his efforts, are worth it.

POINT OF VIEW

Point-of-view in *Gulliver's Travels* shifts. As Gulliver travels, his viewpoint changes. Though the novel is narrated by Gulliver, he is not an omniscient (all-knowing) narrator. Because Swift frequently satirizes Gulliver, we must be on our guard against what Gulliver would have us believe. Sometimes Gulliver speaks for Swift, and sometimes he doesn't. Swift's aim in this book is for you to come to terms with your ideas on some important questions regarding humanity and to be aware of the factors that influence your beliefs. Like all effective teachers, Swift knows that his audience has to learn to think for itself, and not simply accept everything he tells us through his narrator.

FORM AND STRUCTURE

The novel is written in the form of a travel book. Swift chose this device because travel tends to change our perspective on the world around us. What may seem strange at the start of a trip may well seem ordinary by the end, or strange in other ways, for different reasons. As Gulliver voyages, and we voyage with him, his (and our) viewpoint changes according to the place(s) in which he finds himself and the things that happen to him there.

True to form, Swift also satirizes travel books in *Gulliver's Travels*.

The Story

A LETTER FROM CAPTAIN GULLIVER TO HIS COUSIN SYMPSON

This letter, written ten years after Gulliver completed his narrative, is your first introduction to the "author." What a grouch he is! And how peculiarly he speaks—of *Yahoos*, of *Houyhnhnms*, of being made *to say the thing that was not.* Really, he sounds like some sort of crank who has half lost his wits. But pay close attention here, for this letter is full of clues as to how to read this novel and what to watch for in it.

Though the narrative takes the form of a travel book, it's really about England in the time of Swift. We know this because Gulliver complains that a chapter about Queen Anne was inserted into his book. He also says that he has been accused of making fun of important political figures, of degrading human nature, and of abusing the female sex. You know from the outset, then, that the *Travels* aroused (and still arouses) controversy. We still read this book because it is not just about eighteenth-century England, but about man in general.

Gulliver says he did not want to publish his book. This seems odd, since he gave the manuscript to a publisher. Maybe Gulliver was being coy, or maybe he doesn't always tell the truth.

The only point in publishing his book, Gulliver says, would have been to improve mankind. Depending on your view, and on the spirit in which it's undertaken, this is either a very idealistic or presumptuous project. But six months have passed since his book came out, and mankind, says Gulliver, has made no progress. So he concludes that men are beyond correction. As a result, Gulliver is angry, bitter, and disappointed.

Gulliver says he's been corrupted by contact with other *Yahoos* (even by the sound of it, not a complimentary name), especially by his family. You may well be tempted to say, "Fine, Gulliver, who needs you!" Many readers have had this reaction.

THE PUBLISHER TO THE READER

We learn more about Gulliver in Richard Sympson's letter.

Gulliver's first name is Lemuel. In the Bible (Proverbs 31:9) Lemuel says, "Open thy mouth, judge righteously, and plead the cause of the poor and needy." He also speaks in praise of women, and counsels men to honor their wives. Gulliver, at this point, seems a far cry from the biblical Lemuel. As you read the novel think about Swift's reasons for choosing this name. Bear in mind what you already know about satire, and Swiftian satire in particular.

Sympson tells us that Gulliver is well thought of by his neighbors. So perhaps we shouldn't judge him prematurely. Maybe he's having a hard time readjusting after a traumatic period of travel.

Sympson tells us Gulliver gave him *carte blanche* with regard to his manuscript. So it would seem that Gulliver does lie sometimes. After all, he didn't stop the presses.

Even if Gulliver does lie, he isn't irresponsible. His book was so full of facts and so copiously documented that Sympson had to make certain cuts. Sympson offers this as though Gulliver's fondness for facts is evidence that he is interested in the truth, even if he doesn't always tell it. But facts aren't the same thing as truth. What is true? What is truth? These are central questions in this book.

Even if it seems he tells an occasional untruth, Gulliver is an okay guy. Sympson tells you that within "the first pages" of the narrative, Gulliver will prove this to your "satisfaction."

NOTE: Swift didn't write *Gulliver's Travels* so that readers would "receive satisfaction." He said he wrote it "to vex." Keep this in mind. Keep in mind, too, that part of Swift's technique is to keep you guessing. Just as Gulliver doesn't always reflect Swift's views, neither does Sympson, nor do the other characters.

Both of these letters, of course, are fictions invented by Swift. They are good illustrations of another important Swiftian technique. The letters provide a sort of documentation regarding Gulliver's character and the publication of his book. Swift habitually presents fantastical incidents, objects, and perceptions in the form of "official documentation." Take note that Gulliver habitually gives proof—in the form of numerical comparisons, measurements, etc.—when he recounts something outside reality as we know it.

PART I

In this part, Gulliver goes to the land of Lilliput, where people are no more than six inches high, where sheep, horses, and "large" fowl fit in the palm of Gulliver's hand. Dubbed by the Lilliputians as the "Man-Mountain," Gulliver's presence poses such gigantic problems that the government must enact special leg-

islation to deal with such things as Gulliver's diet and
the manner in which his excrement is to be handled.
Swift has come under a lot of fire for his emphasis on
and vivid descriptions of urination, defecation, and
the body in general. Throughout this book Swift juxtaposes Gulliver's physicality and bodily functions
against the ultratidy, picturebook-tiny, form-obsessed
Lilliputians. Many of the Lilliputians' political machinations represent inflamed incidents in the English
politics of Swift's time. As you read this section think
about the things we normally associate with "big" and
"little"—in his allegorical juxtapositions, Swift
makes a pointed exploration of personal and political
grossness, largesse, narrowness, and tyranny.

CHAPTER I

You're really "starting over" as you dive into Chapter I. Right away you know from the startling difference in tone that Gulliver started his voyages with one
viewpoint and finished them with another. Try to put
Gulliver's letter to Richard Sympson in the back of
your mind (but don't forget it entirely). Getting to
know Gulliver will be as much a voyage for you, as his
travels were for him.

Notice how Gulliver tries to make a good impression on you, tries to present himself as solid and
respectable, as though he were applying for a job. He
tells you that his father had a "small Estate in Nottinghamshire," that he was the third of five sons, that he
spent three years at Emanuel College, Cambridge,
that because his family wasn't rich, he stopped formal
schooling and was apprenticed to a Mr. Bates. With
his allowance, he managed to study navigation,
mathematics, and medicine ("physic"), which he
knew would be useful when he began to travel, as he
had always felt he was meant to do. On the basis of

recommendations from Mr. Bates, he was hired as "surgeon" (physician) aboard the *Swallow*, his first ship. Again, on the basis of Mr. Bates' recommendations, Gulliver is able to set up a medical practice upon his return from sea. He marries, his practice flags, and because "conscience would not suffer me to imitate the bad practice of too many among my brethren"— in other words, to steal, swindle, and the like—he resolves to go to sea.

Evidently satisfied by this introduction of himself, Gulliver launches into his tale. It's true that he's given us many details. He not only mentions the name of his home region, college, employers, ships, wife, streets of residence, etc.; he is at pains to furnish us specifics, and wants to make sure we note them. From the outset, then, you know that Gulliver is detail-oriented.

But most of the details Gulliver gives us are such as we might find on his résumé. And what does a résumé tell you about a person? The official, public aspects of his life. This helps us as we try to make a picture of the person. We can infer that Gulliver is conscientious (he used his allowance for his studies), hard working (he seems never to have been out of a job when not in school), and competent (he gets good references). Helpful as these details are, they're still not a full portrait. The only personal information we get from Gulliver is that *compared* to some of his peers, he's honest. Maybe Gulliver needs the impetus of comparison to delve behind his public appearance; certainly it is through comparing Gulliver to those he meets during his voyages that you'll get to know Gulliver.

It is by chance that Gulliver finds himself in Lilliput. In the haze, his ship hits a rock, and Gulliver and some of his mates let down a boat and try to row toward shore. But the wind overturns the boat, and only Gulliver makes it to land. He immediately falls asleep on the grass. The first thing he feels on waking is that his arms, body, and hair are pinned to the ground. Flat on his back, face to the sun, Gulliver is blinded by the light. Bear in mind, as you read, the importance to Gulliver of his eyesight, the lengths to which he'll go to protect it, and the different value the Lilliputians ascribe to vision, Gulliver's in particular.

The first thing Gulliver sees on this strange shore is a human creature six inches high, with a bow and arrow in its hands and a quiver on its back. This creature has walked up Gulliver's leg, stomach, and chest, and stands just in front of his chin. Behind this creature are forty of his fellows.

NOTE: How blasé Gulliver is as he tells us of people six inches high! How detailed is his description! Because Gulliver doesn't question the reality of what he's seeing, we don't either. And because he describes with extreme clarity and care, he earns our confidence and we become "conditioned" to believe the improbable, fantastical things Gulliver recounts. Swift has several techniques that ensure that we'll accept the fantastical. Gulliver's reliable observations in Part I is one such device. But Gulliver, as you'll see, isn't always completely believable, which is why Swift needs recourse to other techniques as well.

Gulliver manages to break his bonds, and as soon as he does, one of the Lilliputians shouts an order and the rest shoot their arrows at Gulliver. In a moment, the tiny ones subdue the giant. (Gulliver lies back, quietly, so as to avoid more arrows.) A work crew arrives and starts building a stage. When it's finished, a person who's obviously a noble arrives and makes Gulliver a long, highly oratorical speech. Gulliver doesn't understand a word, and responds to this show by putting his finger on his mouth and grunting to indicate that he's hungry. What a contrast between the tiny, ceremonial Lilliputian and the grunting hulk who doesn't seem to care about words (much less oratory!) and just wants to be fed. Gulliver calls up images of a beast, or a baby. When he gives us the catalog of all he's eaten, he seems much more like a beast. And it's only after the Lilliputians feed Gulliver that he feels honorbound not to hurt them.

Gulliver realizes his conduct may be against the "strict rules of decency," but he can't help himself. He's overcome by the demands of his body, and in contrast to the refined-seeming Lilliputians, he seems a little less human for it.

When he urinates, the Lilliputians scatter as though from a flood. Not only does Gulliver appear crude, he's positively dangerous, a walking natural disaster! He himself describes his urine as a "torrent which fell with . . . noise and violence." Gulliver's begun looking at himself and his functions through the eyes of his host. Have you?

He's also looking at his hosts with newly awakened eyes. When the emperor orders Gulliver to be transported to his court, the Lilliputians do sophisticated calculations to arrive at the exact amount of wood they will need for Gulliver's cart. They also devise a pulley system to raise Gulliver from the ground to the cart. Gulliver is so impressed he practically begins to brag about the Lilliputians.

They, however, don't hold Gulliver in such high regard. They house him in a polluted temple. Gulliver says he "creeps" inside his lodging, like something nasty and debased.

No doubt Gulliver is experiencing some conflicting feelings. On the one hand, he is the size of a Lilliputian mountain, the mere fact of his presence is a major event. On the other hand, he's crude compared to the Lilliputians, less civilized seeming. How do you think you'd react if you were in Gulliver's shoes?

CHAPTER II

Gulliver starts off with his first description of the land of Lilliput: the countryside is gardenlike, the city genteel enough to recall painted scenery in a theater.

Against this idyll Gulliver juxtaposes a description of his first bowel movement. He says he was caught between "urgency and shame," that he'd waited as long as he could (two days), and that he relieved himself in the temple where the offense to others would be lessened. From that day on, the Lilliputian senate appoints two servants whose job it is to carry away Gulliver's excrement in wheelbarrows.

NOTE: Think for a minute about Swift's purpose here. Again we have an instance of high contrast between Gulliver and his hosts, with Gulliver definitely on the lower end. There's something else. At the end of his defense, Gulliver cites "maligners" who have on this and other occasions called his character into question. This draws us back to Gulliver's letter to Sympson. It also seems to be Swift referring to other of his works (*A Tale of a Tub* and his political writings) that caused a public outcry. You can see here why some readers have concluded that Gulliver is Swift.

We have another example of Gulliver seeing through Lilliputian eyes when he describes the emperor. How odd that Gulliver is impressed by the

tallness of the monarch. He is taller than his subjects
by almost the breadth of Gulliver's fingernail. To the
Lilliputians, this may well be a big difference, but to
Gulliver? What do you think of physical size as a cri-
terion for the power to rule? Start thinking about the
details you're given on Lilliputian government. For
example, what do you think when Gulliver tells you
that government officials are making money on the
side by selling permits to those who wish to have a
look at Gulliver? On the one hand, it's laudable that
the government did something to prevent chaos in
the country (whole villages were being deserted,
lands were being left untended because of the mass
exodus to the capital). On the other, the officials are
obviously corrupt. What's more, Gulliver, who prid-
ed himself on his honesty just a chapter ago, seems
undisturbed.

The government really has its hands full with Gulliver, docile as he is. Council members fear his diet
could cause a famine; the stench of his carcass, were
they to kill him, might pollute the entire city, even
bring on the plague. Good reports on Gulliver's
behavior convince the emperor not to harm him,
however. So it's decreed that Gulliver shall have a suit
of clothes tailored in high Lilliputian style, language
lessons, and sufficient food even though it will require
special additions to the national treasury.

First, though, Gulliver must swear peace to the
kingdom and submit to a personal inventory (to make
sure he has no weapons). The painstaking search Gulliver undergoes represents the suspicions between
the Tories and the Whigs in the first quarter of the
eighteenth century. In 1715 the Earl of Oxford and
Viscount Bolingbroke, leaders of the Tories (by this
time, Swift was also a Tory and a close friend of these
men), were put under gruelling investigations by the

Whigs. Gulliver in Part I has been said to represent Oxford and/or Bolingbroke, and the Lilliputians the suspicious, bureaucratic, power-hungry (Swift's view of them, at any rate) Whigs.

Gulliver—and the Tories—are not such easy marks. Gulliver does not let the Lilliputians into all of his pockets. He manages to keep secret his eyeglasses and a magnifying glass. Let's see how, or if, these instruments keep him safe from his blind spots.

CHAPTER III

In Chapter III we learn some of the "inner workings" of the Lilliputian political system. Bear in mind that Swift is drawing a parallel here to the court of George I.

Political offices frequently become vacant through disgrace. To gain entry into court, candidates petition to entertain the emperor; after he receives five or six such petitions he sets up a competition in which they must all do the Dance on the Rope. Whoever jumps the highest without taking a tumble gets the job. Sometimes chief ministers in midcareer are asked to make a display of their competency; Flimnap (symbolizing Robert Walpole, the leader of the Whigs), the Lilliputian treasurer, is admired for his ability to jump at least an inch higher than his peers. Gulliver tells us that these competitions are often the cause of fatal accidents; Flimnap, in fact, would have killed himself in a recent fall had not one of the king's "cushions" broken his downward flight. The king's "cushion" represents George I's mistress, who aided Walpole in his return to power after a "fall."

It's easy to see that Lilliputian politics have their fair share of absurdity and menace. How on earth does rope jumping qualify one to hold office? That an emperor would base his hiring system on a practice proven to be injurious to many of the candidates is appalling. That great numbers of people crowd to the capital to watch these "diversions" is horrifying.

NOTE: By ostensibly talking about the Lilliputians Swift is able to make a devastating case against the Whigs. Swift could have never made such bold accusations had he actually "named names." Satire is indeed a powerful tool.

Gulliver has been growing increasingly impatient to be unchained. The matter is hotly debated in council, where it is first decided that Gulliver must swear allegiance in the Lilliputian manner (hold his right foot in his left hand, place the middle finger of his right hand on the crown of his head, and his thumb on the tip of his right ear) to the terms set for his "full liberty." What ridiculous ceremony, but Gulliver complies.

Let's take a look at the conditions for Gulliver's freedom. The document begins with a full paragraph of some of the most overblown praise of a ruler you or I have ever read. Gulliver must perform many tasks for the kingdom, ranging from messenger to surveyor to raiser of stones, and "do his utmost to destroy" the Blefuscudian fleet. Otherwise (!), Gulliver is at "full liberty."

Gulliver reacts by prostrating himself before the emperor. Perhaps this is what captivity in a strange land would do to any of us.

CHAPTER IV

We get further comparisons between Lilliput and England. Reldresal, a Lilliputian government officer (who represents Walpole's successor), pays Gulliver a special visit. His purpose is to acquaint Gulliver further with domestic and international politics, and to enlist Gulliver's aid. There is, he says, "a violent faction at home [corresponding to the Tories], and the danger of an invasion by a most potent enemy [representing France] from abroad."

In Lilliput, the warring parties are the High-Heels (the Tories) and the Low-Heels (the Whigs). Just as George I favored the Whigs, so the Lilliputian emperor favors the Low-Heels. Just as George I's successor, the Prince of Wales, indicated favor to both parties, the Lilliputian heir to the throne wears one high heel and one low.

Blefuscu is the "other great empire of the universe," says Reldresal, and is preparing an invasion. As Lilliput here stands for England, so Blefuscu stands for France; from 1701 to 1713 these two countries were engaged in the War of the Spanish Succession. Again in a parallel to Europe, the war between Lilliput and Blefuscu began because of religious differences, represented by the manner in which eggs are broken before being eaten. It used to be that everyone broke the larger end of the egg. One day, however, when the emperor was a child, he cut his finger on the shell. His father immediately issued an edict that all subjects would from then on break the smaller end of their eggs, or suffer severe penalties. There were rebellions throughout the kingdom so intense that one emperor lost his life, another his crown. The fire was stoked from *agents provocateurs* from Blefuscu. When the rebellions finally came to an end, many Big-Endians went into exile in Blefuscu. To this day in Lilliput the books of the Big-Endians are outlawed and no member of this sect is permitted to have a government job. Lilliputians are bitter that Blefuscudians consider them to have started a religious schism.

NOTE: The Big-Endians represent the Roman Catholics, the Little-Endians, Protestants. The Emperor's edict corresponds to Henry VIII's edict denying the authority of the pope. The Lilliputian emperor who lost his life in the rebellions corresponds to Charles I, who was executed; the Lilliputian emperor who lost his crown corresponds to James II, who went into forced exile, after which Catholics living in England were put under severe restrictions.

The differences between Big-Endians and Little-Endians seem so petty, yet the consequences of these differences are the horrors of war and civil strife. Surely Swift wants us to see the differences between Catholics and Protestants in this light. Remember, Swift was a high-ranking Protestant cleric who wanted the Church of England to have a strong footing even in Ireland (predominantly Catholic). One might expect him to side with the Little-Endians. In his fiercely satiric way Swift is putting humanitarian concerns over sectarian concerns. Religious differences, he seems to be saying, are finally small, and not worth going to war over.

Gulliver here is blind to Swift's wisdom (a good argument if you hold that Gulliver is not Swift). He tells Reldresal that though it would be inappropriate for him, as a foreigner, to meddle in domestic politics, he promises "with the hazard of my life, to defend [the emperor's] person and state against all invaders." Can it be that Gulliver really identifies with the Little-Endians? Or is it that Gulliver wishes to prove that he's not the monster the Lilliputians consider him to be.

In the course of his political lecture, Reldresal tells Gulliver, " . . . as to what we have heard you affirm, that there are other kingdoms and states in the world inhabited by human creatures as large as yourself, our philosophers are in much doubt, and would rather conjecture that you dropped from the moon, or one of the stars; because it is certain, that a hundred mortals of your bulk would, in a short time, destroy all the fruits and cattle of his majesty's dominions."

Perhaps Gulliver just wants to express his gratitude for the Lilliputians electing to feed, clothe, and shelter him. How backward, it seems, that in order to do so he must promise to fight in a war. And for whom? For the Lilliputians, who are beginning to seem as mentally small as they are physically diminutive. Gulliver doesn't see this yet, but he'll begin to toward the end of the next chapter.

CHAPTER V

Anxious not to lose what freedom he has, Gulliver walks across the harbor and seizes the Blefuscudian fleet. He unties each boat from its mooring, ties the boats together so that they form a sort of seafaring train, and strides back to Lilliput with the fleet literally in hand. Gulliver succeeds in spite of the bow and arrow attacks of the Blefuscudians. Had he not stopped his work for a moment to put on his eyeglasses, he would have been blinded. Keep this detail in mind as you read about Gulliver's downfall in Lilliput.

Immediately upon his return to Lilliput Gulliver is given the land's highest title of honor, *Nardac*. The emperor confides to Gulliver that he plans to colonize Blefuscu and govern it himself. Of course, the Blefuscudian Big-Endians will be destroyed. Gulliver protests, says he "would never be an instrument of bringing a free and brave people into slavery . . . " For

Gulliver in Lilliput, this is the beginning of the end. But he still doesn't see it.

He continues in the service of his own ideals of fairness. When ambassadors from Blefuscu arrive to offer a humble treaty of peace, Gulliver intercedes on their behalf so that the final treaty will be more equitable. (The Lilliputians did, after all, attack without warning; and because they had Gulliver, against whom the Blefuscudians didn't stand a chance, they never even engaged their own soldiers.) The Blefuscudians express their gratitude to Gulliver by inviting him to their court. The Lilliputian emperor grants permission for this trip, but coldly. Flimnap tells Gulliver straight out that the emperor considered Gulliver's dealings with the Blefuscudians a "mark of disaffection." Gulliver's response? "This was the first time I began to conceive some imperfect idea of courts and ministers."

Swift, you well know, has long been concerned with unjust politics, and the events in this chapter refer to events in England. Gulliver's capture of the Blefuscudian fleet refers to the events leading up to the Treaty of Utrecht (1713), which ended the War of Spanish Succession between England and France. This treaty was introduced by the Tories; Gulliver's "mark of disaffection" stands for the Whig contentions that the treaty was too easy on France. For their part, the Tories were satisfied that England had dominion over the sea.

NOTE: As you've probably guessed, Gulliver here stands for Oxford and Bolingbroke, the Tory leaders. Notice how involved Swift's satire is, though. Gulliver is used on both sides—it is he who is the physical aggressor against Blefuscu as well as their "ally" when it comes to making a peace treaty. Little wonder that critics have puzzled for years over the boundaries between Swift's identity and Gulliver's.

After all this, Gulliver is nonetheless glad when he has the opportunity to do the emperor a favor. When he's awakened by a crowd at his door telling him the royal apartment is on fire, he rushes over, and urinates into the royal chambers. Within three minutes Gulliver saves the palace. The empress, however, refuses to set foot in her apartment and vows revenge against Gulliver. The empress here represents Queen Anne, who reacted against Swift's earlier *A Tale of a Tub* in much the way the empress reacted to Gulliver's urinating in her home. Queen Anne blocked Swift's advancement in the Church of England.

NOTE: What do you think of Gulliver's solution? Certainly it was quick and effective. The Lilliputians evidently had confidence in Gulliver's resourcefulness because they rushed to seek his help. Had Gulliver done something on a Lilliputian scale the palace would have burned to the ground. Gulliver was really stuck. Had he failed to douse the fire, the queen would also have sworn revenge. Gulliver's solution was far from genteel, but so is a raging fire. Gross problems often require gross measures. Finally it all depends on your definition of "gross."

Stop for a moment and think about Gulliver. In Chapter III he prostrated himself before the emperor, thankful for his dubious freedom. Here, though, he's acted with admirable independence, and has proved himself faithful to appealing notions of justice, fairness, and graciousness in victory. Gulliver seems to be one of "the good guys." Would you agree?

CHAPTER VI

In this chapter we get more of Gulliver's perceptions on the Lilliputians, and a fine example of one of
Swift's most effective techniques.

Gulliver tells us that there is "an exact proportion"
between the size of Lilliputian humans and animals,
birds, trees, vegetables, etc. "Nature," he tells us,
"hath adapted the eyes of the Lilliputians to all objects
proper for their view: they see with great exactness,
but at no great distance." To illustrate this point, he
tells us he has seen "a young girl threading an invisible needle with invisible silk." Notice the interplay
here between the literal and the figurative.

NOTE: This is one of Swift's most important satirical techniques, and it works on us in two ways. We
accept the information pertaining to the literal because
it is laid out for us *precisely* with consistent-seeming
comparisons. We have confidence in Gulliver at this
point because he has taken pains to give us lots of
details: he seems like a character who's "done his
homework." Because the literal seems to hold up, it
smoothes our way as we slide over into the figurative.
Gulliver gives us supporting evidence both before and
after. Yet, would the Lilliputians need good eyesight
to see such tiny animals? they are all on the same
scale; to Gulliver, Lilliputian thread may be invisible,
but it isn't to them. Gulliver's laps is deliberate on the
part of Swift. Swift is able to subtly satirize Gulliver
even as Gulliver is telling us something important,
perceptive, and true about the Lilliputians. Their
views are so narrow they can't be said to see at "great
distance." As readers of Swiftian satire, we must be
alert to the fact that it cuts more than one way.

As we read on, we can't help but be further impressed with the correctness of Gulliver's assessment of Lilliputian "vision." He tells us that a person who accuses another of a crime of which the latter is found to be innocent, is immediately put to a cruel death, and the unjustly accused is rewarded materially. Not only that, he receives a title of distinction from the emperor. From what you already know of the workings of the Lilliputian court, how much confidence do you have in the legal system here? At the very least, many crimes must go unreported.

And anyone here who obeys the laws for "seventy-three moons" is rewarded with a title of honor and a goodly sum of money. The Lilliputians find it odd that in Gulliver's country the judiciary system is based mainly on punishment. This is an interesting point, but do you think the Lilliputians would make such a big deal of staying within the laws if nearly everyone did so?

Gulliver expounds on Lilliputian hiring practices. You have already seen the importance of rope jumping and other such skills in the attainment of public office. Morals, believe the Lilliputians, count more than abilities, since those with high intelligence are usually lacking in moral virtues. Mistakes made in ignorance, reason the Lilliputians, usually have less serious consequences than those made by corrupt cunning. What do you think? Is intelligence to be feared? To be punished so? And what of "moral virtue"? It seems that in Lilliput this translates as utter servitude to the emperor. No one who rejects the notion of the divine right of kings is allowed to hold public office. What about the free flow of ideas? Do you think insuring against such freedom of belief is a sign of a healthy society and a secure government? What do you think Swift thinks?

For all their display of logic, the Lilliputians show themselves to be very illogical. Ingratitude is considered a heinous crime because "whoever makes ill returns to his benefactor, must needs be a common enemy to the rest of mankind . . . and therefore . . . not fit to live." Ingratitude is not an appealing trait, but the reasoning here is cockeyed. Being guilty of ingratitude on one occasion does not signal that a person is a menace to society at large. And an awful lot of offenses in Lilliput are punished by death. How do you feel about this?

The Lilliputians also show themselves to be cynical with regard to love and families. A child is never under any obligation to his parents for conceiving and begetting him, since life is no great bargain anyway, and because his or her parents were just acting out of lust. Children are sent away to school and see their parents only twice a year. Girls receive schooling inferior to that for boys. And unless you're born into the upper class, you have no choice as to what to study. Lower-class kids are assigned a trade and that's it. The poorest of the poor have no option but to tend the land, if their parents have any.

Still, Gulliver retains his admiration of Lilliputian ingenuity. They determine what size to make his clothes by measuring only his right thumb—twice around the thumb, they calculate, is once around the wrist, and "so on to the neck and waist." You're left on your own to make an assessment of the Lilliputians (and of Gulliver). Gulliver may well be less offended by the Lilliputians than is Swift. This, too, is one of Swift's ways of making sure you stand on your own two feet while reading this book. Even though Gulliver's your tour guide, you should feel free to question what he tells you.

For all his docility, Gulliver is not on solid footing with his hosts. A rumor has circulated that the wife of the treasurer has been paying secret visits to Gulliver. The treasurer is livid at what he supposes to be his wife's infidelity. It's hard not to laugh out loud at such a ridiculous suspicion. Yet Gulliver dare not, because for him this means big trouble.

CHAPTER VII

Gulliver has worn out his welcome in Lilliput. He receives a "secret visit" from a government official who tells him that the emperor and the council are preparing a list of articles for Gulliver's impeachment for high treason. The charges are: 1. urinating in a public place; 2. having refused to destroy all the Blefuscudians who wouldn't forsake the "Big-Endian heresy"; 3. having helped the Blefuscudians with the terms of the peace treaty; 4. preparing to go to Blefuscu, for which the emperor has given only verbal permission.

Some in the council, including the treasurer and the admiral, insist that Gulliver immediately be put to a painful death. Their plan was to set Gulliver's house afire and then shoot him with poisonous arrows as he tried to escape. His sheets and clothes would already have been treated with a poison that would have him tearing his flesh. What do you think of this? Even if you believe the Lilliputians have a claim against Gulliver punishable by death, what do you think of their form of capital punishment?

After debate, the council decides instead to blind Gulliver, as a mark of their "lenity" (mercy). But let's look for a minute at the debate that preceded this decision. Some ministers argued that when blinded, certain fowl eat more than before. If this should happen to Gulliver, his diet might well cause a famine for everyone else in Lilliput. Another suggestion was to starve Gulliver to death—this way the treasury wouldn't be exhausted, and Gulliver's corpse wouldn't smell so bad as it would if he were well fed at the end. It would, of course, carry a stench; so they'd chop his body into little pieces and bury it in the far corners of the kingdom. The plan adopted is to put out Gulliver's eyes:

> That the loss of your eyes would be no impediment to your bodily strength, by which you might still be useful to his Majesty. That blindness is an addition to courage, by concealing dangers from us; that the fear you had for your eyes was the greatest difficulty in bringing over the enemy's fleet; and it would be sufficient for you to see by the eyes of the ministers, since the greatest princes do no more.

No mention is made in the public records of the plan to starve Gulliver.

NOTE: Compare the importance of sight as held by the Lilliputians, Gulliver, and Swift. For the Lilliputians sight approaches blindness. We learn at this point that "lenity," in the same way, is nearer to what we normally consider punishment. Gulliver's visitor observes that shows of the emperor's "lenity" were much feared, "that the more these praises were enlarged and insisted on, the more inhuman was the punishment, and the sufferer more innocent." Gulliver says, "I was so ill a judge of things, that I could not discover the lenity and favour of this sentence. . . ." He's right—there is no lenity in his sentence—and mistaken in doubting his own judgment.

Gulliver is careful to give us detailed reports of what he sees. In fact, he gets lost in the literal. Swift, by playing with literal perspective—big, little; animal, human; etc.—expands the vision of our mind's eye.

Gulliver resolves to flee to Blefuscu, which corresponds to Bolingbroke's fleeing to France just before his trial.

CHAPTER VIII

While Gulliver is in Blefuscu, the Lilliputian emperor sends a request that Gulliver be returned bound hand and foot to Lilliput to receive his punishment. The Blefuscudian ruler refuses, and offers Gulliver complete protection for the rest of his life.

But Gulliver resolves to return to England. He stays there just two months, "insatiable" as he is to see foreign countries.

NOTE: What do you think of Gulliver? Considering what he's been through, he seems to be a solid character. He isn't cruel, though he's been treated cruelly; he isn't violent, though he's been dealt with violently; and he isn't crafty, though he's been dealt some rude blows by Lilliputian cunning. Gulliver seems as naïve as he is good; perhaps, he's good because he's naïve. It is his finer qualities of character, rather than his physical size, that lend Gulliver stature while he's in Lilliput.

PART II

The tables are turned on Gulliver when he reaches Brobdingnag. Here the natives are giants, and Gulliver begins to think of himself as Lilliputian. Throughout the book he is constantly afraid of being injured, and indeed he is often hurt; his feelings of insecurity give rise to other feelings we have not seen in Gulliver before, notably disgust, violence, and shame.

CHAPTER I

Gulliver's ship gets blown off course by a huge storm. You may notice that Gulliver's description of this is almost impossible to follow. Swift is satirizing specialist language, nautical jargon in particular. After all the East North Easts and South South Wests, he seems to be saying, you lose all sense of direction.

When an island appears, a group of sailors including Gulliver goes off to explore it. Gulliver leaves the group to do some looking around on his own. After a while he sees his mates running for their boat, pursued by a "monster." The sailors make their getaway, but Gulliver is left on this island of monsters.

He is sure he will die here, and for the first time Gulliver yearns mournfully for his family. "I reflected," says Gulliver, "what a mortification it must prove to me to appear as inconsiderable in this nation as one single Lilliputian would be among us." At this point he has enough presence of mind to realize that such prideful thoughts are ridiculous at such a time. For, he reasons, he'll probably end up a "morsel in the mouth of the first among these enormous barbarians. . . ."

A Brobdingnagian reaper approaches and Gulliver screams for all he is worth so he won't be trampled underfoot. The "monster" inspects Gulliver, Gulliver tells us, as though he were "a small dangerous animal!" much as he himself has done with a "weasel in England." Gulliver feels sure the reaper will dash him to the ground "as we usually do with any little hateful animal." Later Gulliver likens himself to a "toad," a "spider," a "kitten," and a "puppy-dog." His self-image is really taking a beating. Why? Because he appears small.

The reaper, however, doesn't harm Gulliver, recognizing that the tiny creature can speak and gesticulate, and recognizing too that he is frightened. So maybe the giant is not such a "monster." The reaper brings Gulliver to the farmer, who takes him home. His family places Gulliver on the table where he bows, speaks, gesticulates, offers his entire purse of gold (the farmer doesn't recognize the pieces as coins, so tiny are they), kisses the farmer's hand to thank him for not allowing his son to harm him. Gulliver is "performing" like a minuscule freak in a circus.

After dinner the mother nurses her baby. "I must confess," says Gulliver, "no object ever disgusted me so much as the sight of her monstrous breast. . . ." He goes on to give us an unsettling description of this six-foot breast. Gulliver reflects on the "fair skins of our English ladies, who appear so beautiful to us, only because they are of our own size." He remembers, too, that the Lilliputians, when they looked at him close up, were disgusted by the coarseness of his skin and features.

Here is another first in Gulliver's narrative. Awakened by rats during a dream of his family, he is so startled, frightened, disoriented (he says the rats are the size of bulldogs), and disgusted, that he kills one of them. You can argue that this is self-defense, but what about Gulliver stabbing the other rat in the back as he is escaping? That is the low-down rage of someone who feels impotent.

NOTE: In Part I Gulliver felt no shame about his bodily functions, even after he was impeached for urinating in public. Here his language is euphemistic regarding excretion ("I was pressed to more than one thing, which another could not do for me"), and he takes care to hide himself between sorrel leaves so that no one will see him as he "discharged the necessities of nature" (another euphemism). He then apologizes to *you* for making mention of this at all, and justifies himself by saying that his only interest in writing up his voyages is in "truth." Yet what a defensive apology it is. He addresses you as "gentle reader" but raises the possibility that you have a "grovelling vulgar" mind.

Gulliver—scared, disoriented, disgusted—anticipates criticism and can't keep himself from lashing out.

CHAPTER II

Gulliver literally becomes a freak in this chapter. He is given the baby's cradle—comfortable, but how would you feel sleeping in a cradle?—for a bed. Gulliver is "turned over" to the farmer's daughter, who cares for him in much the same way that she cares for her doll. In fact, her name for Gulliver, *Grildrig*, means mannikin. Gulliver's name for the girl is *Glumdalclitch*, which in Brobdingnagian means little nurse. An odd name, since compared to Gulliver she is a giant. But maybe Gulliver isn't feeling at all well.

Much against Glumdalclitch's will, her father has Gulliver give public shows. He is put on a table where he shows off his knowledge of the local language,

drinks from a thimble, flourishes his (to them, minia-
ture) sword, vaults with the aid of a piece of straw. In
short, he does all the things that people do, except on
a toy scale. Gulliver is a great sensation, and the farmer, who's really raking it in, takes Gulliver on the
road.

In the England of Swift's time it was common for
abnormal people to be put on display. Think of The
Elephant Man, for instance. You can't help but empa-
thize with Gulliver here; obviously Swift thinks this
sort of human "carnaval act" is shameful.

CHAPTER III

The road show life is just about killing Gulliver and
his Master (Gulliver's name for the farmer, who is,
after all, a peasant). How subservient Gulliver has
become. Think of the crank who wrote the letter to his
publisher.

Gulliver's life is saved when the king and queen of
Brobdingnag buy him from the farmer after Gulliver
pleads his case in the most humble fashion imagin-
able. He bows, scrapes, pledges undying loyalty, and
embraces the tip of the queen's finger.

The king sends for eminent scholars to examine
Gulliver. They conclude that he is in fact a freak of
nature. Gulliver finds this "a determination exactly
agreeable to the modern philosophy of Europe"
where professors have invented the category of
"freak" as a cover for their own ignorance when they
come on something that stymies them. This is Swift
taking a shot at the academics of his day. Freaks are
treated more kindly in Brobdingnag than in Europe,
though, for Gulliver is outfitted with a luxurious box
by the best court artisans to serve as his home.

The king, after talking with Gulliver about European ways, concludes that not only is Gulliver a freak, but he comes from a freakish society as well. Gulliver's stories of Whigs and Tories make the king laugh out loud and exclaim, "how contemptible a thing was human grandeur, which could be mimicked by such diminutive insects" as Gulliver. At first Gulliver is indignant to hear his "noble country, the mistress of arts and arms, the scourge of France, the arbitress of Europe, the seat of virtue, piety, honour and truth, the pride and envy of the world, so contemptuously treated."

This hardly matches the attitudes of the Gulliver who wrote the letter that opens this novel. His overblown language here is an indication of his defensiveness.

Gulliver's ego can't take this for long. He suspects that were he to see his English compatriots now, he would laugh at them just the way the Brobdingnagians laugh at him. He can't help but smile when he sees himself so "ridiculous" in a mirror. "I really began," he says, "to imagine myself dwindled many degrees below my usual size." His perspective is suffering in more ways than one.

Adding insult to injury is the queen's dwarf, who lords it over Gulliver for being so small. Again you see Gulliver's outraged disorientation, for he disdains the dwarf for being a mere thirty feet tall. But the dwarf has his ways of getting revenge—he drops Gulliver into a bowl of cream in which he nearly drowns, and squeezes him into the wedge of a marrow bone. It seems Swift is telling us that pride goeth before a fall.

The queen teases Gulliver for being so fearful, and concludes that his compatriots must all be cowardly. Gulliver is terrified and sickened by Brobdingnagian flies and wasps. Where the queen is oblivious to their excrement and other droppings, to Gulliver this falling matter is torrential. In his agitated state of mind Gulliver seems to overstate his case here. Bird droppings are indeed unpleasant, but they aren't as nightmarish as Gulliver would have us believe. He gets two types of revenge against these giant insects: some he cuts into bits as they fly past; others he displays as freaks when he gets back to England.

Shame, disgust, violence, vengefulness—these are Gulliver's reactions when his pride is steadily attacked. How do you think you would react in similar circumstances?

CHAPTER IV

Telling us about his revenge seems to have calmed Gulliver down a bit, for in this chapter his tone is for the most part dispassionate and his observations reliable. He has two notable lapses, however. One is when a crowd of Brobdingnagians crowd up to his carriage to get a glimpse of him. One woman had a cancer in her breast full of holes so large he could have crept inside them. A man, he tells us, had a wen in his neck larger than five woolpacks; another had a wooden leg twenty feet high. Gulliver says he could see lice rooting through their garments "like swine." Again, he is literally sickened with disgust.

Another example in this chapter of Gulliver's disturbed sense of proportions is when seeing the temple, about which he has heard a great deal, he is disappointed as it is merely 3,000 feet high.

CHAPTER V

Gulliver really takes a beating in this chapter. After teasing the dwarf about dwarf apple trees (which, of course, are huge in Brobdingnag), the dwarf shakes the branches so that the enormous apples pelt Gulliver. Again we see Gulliver's pride and ill-spirited humor punished.

A dog mistakes Gulliver for a doll and takes him in his mouth and runs with him to his master. Gulliver is traumatized, needless to say. Shortly afterward he attends an execution with great interest. He compares the spurts of blood as the man is decapitated as more spectacular than the fountains at Versailles. What a curious, and unfeeling, comparison.

Gulliver is often sent to the maids at court, who play with him as though he were a doll. Their antics, however, are decidedly lascivious. They strip Gulliver, examine him all over; they undress in his presence; they even urinate in front of him. One of the maids picks Gulliver up and places him so that he's sitting astride her nipple. At this, Gulliver finally protests, and is spared further visits with her. He's sick of the maids using him "without any manner of ceremony, like a creature who had no sort of consequence."

The most dangerous thing that happened to him in Brobdingnag, Gulliver tells us, was when a monkey kidnapped him, mistaking him for a baby monkey. Holding him like one of its young, the monkey climbs up to a high roof and feeds Gulliver from its own mouth. Gulliver is rescued, finally, but is so bruised and upset by the event he stays in bed for two weeks. Remember, this is a man who has survived two shipwrecks and after those didn't take to his bed.

The king makes fun of Gulliver and his recent misadventures. This enrages Gulliver, and discourages him, and he reflects "how vain an attempt it is for a man to endeavour doing himself honour among those who are out of all degree of equality or comparison with him." What do you think of Gulliver's conclusion? He's been so battered of late that he equates physical parity with equality.

The chapter ends with Gulliver again being punished for his pride. While out walking he sees a pile of cow dung. He tries to leap over it, a foolish attempt, you're probably saying to yourself. And right you are, for Gulliver lands in the middle of it, or as he says in his newfound shameful modesty, he is "filthily bemired."

CHAPTER VI

This is a very important chapter, both in terms of theme and the techniques Swift employs to express his meanings.

The first thing Gulliver does is to ask the queen for some hairs from her head. With these he makes chairs similar to English cane-backed chairs. They are teeny-tiny from the standpoint of the royal couple, but they keep them nonetheless as souvenirs. They suggest that Gulliver use them as furniture, but he "would rather die a thousand deaths than place a dishonourable part of my body on those precious hairs. . . ." Keep this in mind as you read the rest of this chapter.

The king is curious about Gulliver's country, and asks him lots of questions about it. Gulliver gives quite a detailed account of how things are done in England.

The king is horrified. He can't understand the English system of taxation, and suggests that Gulliver's figures are all wrong, for the country seems headed for bankruptcy. Deficit spending makes no sense at all to the king. Neither does having colonies, unless it's for purposes of self-protection. He's also mystified by England's having a standing army in peacetime. He's astonished that religious differences give rise to problems. And gambling—what a crazy pastime! Gulliver tells us "He was perfectly astonished with the historical account I gave him of our affairs during the last century, protesting it was only an heap of conspiracies, rebellions, murders, massacres, revolutions, banishments, the very worst effects that avarice, faction, hypocrisy, perfidiousness, cruelty, rage, madness, hatred, envy, lust, malice, or ambition could produce."

The king says that though he likes Gulliver, he must conclude that his compatriots are "the most pernicious race of little odious vermin that nature ever suffered to crawl upon the surface of the earth."

In Lilliput it was Gulliver who denigrated England. When he did, we sided with him. But this time things are different. By Gulliver's refusing to sit on the chairs he made, we know that he holds the king and queen in high regard. And with good reason. The royal couple has been good to him. And the king's objections to Gulliver's account of English practices are human, and his comments are delivered gently, without malice. Therefore, we lend credence to the king's assessment of England. Now when we hear England being criticized, we feel that our hands are being slapped. Is it maybe Swift who is rapping our wrists?

NOTE: We feel that our hands are being slapped because we're still identifying with Gulliver. This is natural, as he is the protagonist of this novel. Also, since the king doesn't lump Gulliver with other English people, Gulliver, and we, are able to keep some semblance of self-respect. This is another way in which Swift makes sure we don't become alienated from Gulliver at this point. Even though Gulliver has, in a sense, dug his own grave in this chapter.

CHAPTER VII

The most important thing that happens in this chapter is that we stop identifying with Gulliver as we did before.

Gulliver changes his tune. He tells us he included the material in Chapter VI only out of an "extreme love of truth," and that he was greatly pained by the king's comments. He says also that his account wasn't strictly "historical," but that he "artfully eluded many of his questions, and gave to every point a more favourable turn by many degrees than the strictness of truth would allow." He goes on to compare himself to Dionysius Halicarnassensis in an effort to prove his loyalty to his mother country. Dionysius, however, was an ancient Greek writer who lived in Rome and in his work tried to convince his countrymen that Rome was superior to Greece. So Gulliver tells us once that he has lied; and Swift turns his satire against Gulliver to again undermine his claims on the truth. No doubt you're beginning to be on your guard against what Gulliver tells you.

Gulliver tries to discredit the king's criticisms by calling attention to the seclusion in which he lives, and the resulting narrowness of his thinking. Gulliver isn't forthright, though; he says we should "make allowances" for the king. This is oily condescension. And when he says that "countries of Europe are wholly exempted" from such ignorance you can't help but exclaim over Gulliver's ridiculous vanity and narrow-mindedness. He is guilty of the very trait for which he's criticizing the king.

To prove his case against the monarch, Gulliver recounts his description and offer of gunpowder to the king. The ruler is horrified and for the first time is harsh with Gulliver, calling him an "impotent and groveling" insect. It is hard not to agree with the king, especially since Gulliver has bragged about the ability of gunpowder to dash out people's brains.

Gulliver retaliates by calling attention to examples of what he claims is the king's "ignorance." His instances, however, are of practices that seem altogether reasonable, such as the prohibition of commentaries that make laws less rather than more clear. Swift again turns his satire against Gulliver when Gulliver is telling us how inadequate he finds the king's library. He describes the way in which he is forced to read the books there—the image you get is one of an insect crawling over a majestic tome. Here it seems Swift is reinforcing the king's earlier comment about Gulliver.

CHAPTER VIII

Gulliver's liberation from Brobdingnag comes about through a spectacular accident. Gulliver had been feeling for a while that the kindness he received from the royal couple and the court "ill became the dignity of human kind." He feels more like a puppy than a human adult.

While out one day with the king and queen, an eagle takes Gulliver's box in his beak, flies with him for a while, and then drops him into the sea. Gulliver is rescued by an English ship.

Gulliver reminds us that while in Brobdingnag he couldn't bear to look at himself in the mirror—he appeared ridiculously insignificant. Now, faced with people his own size for the first time in a long while, he can't bear to look at them. The sailors were the most "contemptible creatures I had ever beheld," he tells us. No matter that they just saved his life.

NOTE: It might seem that Gulliver is self-aware when he says "I winked at my own littleness as people do at their own faults." What he misses is that his littleness of spirit and of mind has been his fault while in Brobdingnag.

So blind, disoriented, and ego-bruised is he that he thinks of himself as Brobdingnagian and his English compatriots as Lilliputians. Given the two extremes, wouldn't you choose to be identified with the Brobdingnagians? Gulliver goes so far as to call out to travelers to get out of his way so they don't get trampled. His friends and faimly think he's lost his wits. Do you?

PART III

In Part III Swift is concerned mainly with attacking extreme devotion to theoretical reasoning at the expense of the practical demands of living. His satire is directed toward what he felt was the dogmatism of the scientific community of his time, and against certain political practices and events he found objectionable. Swift's comments about *extreme* devotion to one way of thinking and/or to one favored discipline apply not only to his own time and country. As you read Part III think about the value of scientific research, the value of applied science, and when and how they should overlap.

Of the four parts that compromise the *Travels*, Part III was written last. Perhaps because Swift had used the character of Gulliver to its fullest extent in Parts I, II, and IV, Gulliver is altogether less of a character in this part. In the first two parts, many things happened *to him*; here he describes ways of life that finally have little effect on him. Swift's satire is presented directly to you the reader.

CHAPTER I

Gulliver is captured, then abandoned, by pirates. While out walking near the cave in which he had slept, Gulliver is alarmed by the sudden darkening of the sky, caused by the appearance in front of the sun of a flying island. (Flying islands were staples in the science fiction of Swift's time.) It descends near Gulliver, the inhabitants throw down a pulley-driven chain, and Gulliver is hauled up. So begins his stay on Laputa.

CHAPTER II

The Laputans' appearance—one eye turned inward and the other up to the sky—is symbolic of their activities. Wholly devoted to abstract science, mathematics, and music, they have one eye turned in on their mental activity and one eye fixed on the stars. (Astronomy is a favorite of theirs.) Laputans are so oblivious to those around them that they employ "flappers" whose job it is to give them a flap on the mouth and eyes to let them know someone is talking to them. Just by the appearance Swift gives the Laputans, he lets you know he thinks them pretty silly.

Gulliver interprets Laputa as meaning "flying island." This is one of Swift's foils, though. In Spanish, "la puta" means "the whore," which Swift certainly knew and deliberately made use of. Keep this in mind when you consider the odd ways in which Laputans satisfy their physical needs. Husbands generally ignore their wives, and it is common for wives to meet their lovers in the presence of their husbands. Once a Laputan woman leaves the flying island, she rarely returns. Gulliver even recounts the tale of a woman who ran away from her husband to live with a cruel, deformed footman, so odious did she find her spouse and his Laputan ways.

For all the Laputans' expertise in theoretical matters, their mastery of practical tasks leaves much to be desired. They make Gulliver, after many calculations and measurements, a suit of ill-fitting clothes. Because Laputans disdain geometry, practical discipline that it is, their houses are poorly built because they refuse to use the right angles in their construction.

Though they are given to theoretical thinking, the Laputans are curiously irrational. They are superstitious, believing that you can tell fortunes by the stars. They are also plagued with what may well seem to you—and certainly did to Swift—ridiculous fears having mostly to do with the movement of planets and stars. One such is that the earth was nearly burned by the last comet. Swift offers these specific fears as satire of the speculations of certain scientists of his time.

CHAPTER III

The long, involved description of the physical intricacies of the flying island is another instance of Swift providing "documentation" for something outlandish. The superdetailed, rather dull and wooden description of the flying island and what makes it fly is Swift's parody of the typical paper published in *Transactions*, the journal of the Royal Society. The Royal Society was and is made up of scientists and academics engaged in research. Swift thought a lot of experiments underwritten in his time by the Society frivolous in the extreme. You'll see more stringent proof of this later.

Think back to the Brobdingnagian style of government. When the king of Laputa has to handle rebellious subjects—a problem the king of Brobdingnag never faces, since he has no colonies—he has two means of quelling the insurrection. He can keep the island hovering over the troublesome town(s) so that they are deprived of sunlight and rain. This has comparatively mild consequences, "death and diseases." He can also have the island descend directly onto the region, crushing all life there. The king seldom resorts to this, however, because he wouldn't want to be deprived the riches of his colonies, and more important, he wouldn't want to damage the underside of the island. Contrast this to the Brobdingnagian way of rule.

Gulliver tells us of an incident that almost put an end to the Laputan monarchy. Lindalino, a city within the kingdom, was in revolt against the monarch. At the center of the city, they erected a tower, on top of which was a lodestone piled with a "most combustible fuel" which would burn the island if it came too near.

NOTE: The four paragraphs recounting this incident were excised from all versions of the *Travels* until 1899, for fear of government reprisals against Swift.

The Lindalino (this city stands for Dublin) incident is an allegorical account of the Irish campaign against the introduction of a debased currency (dubbed in Swift's letters against the project "the most combustible fuel," meaning that it would ignite a huge rebellion) into Ireland. An ironmonger by the name of William Wood had obtained permission for his project from George I. The project never went through, owing in great measure to Swift's outraged public letters.

CHAPTER IV

Gulliver gets sick of Laputa, complaining that the inhabitants paid too little attention to him since he's universed in music and mathematics. He goes to Balnibarbi.

There, Gulliver is hosted by Lord Munodi, whose name Swift may have taken from the Latin *mundum odi* ("I hate the world"). Some critics believe that the Lord represents Oxford and/or Bolingbroke. These men were out of step with the tenor of their times, but Swift was a close friend of theirs and admired them both.

Lord Munodi lives in a gorgeous palace with beautifully cultivated grounds. Not far from where he lives, however, are lands that lie fallow. The Academy of Projectors (a projector is someone given to impractical and visionary projects, and the academy is a parody of the Royal Society) had taken charge of the lands on which nothing would grow—their state is an indication of their agricultural "state of the art." Projectors' houses are also built according to "the most advanced formulas" (Swift's irony is obvious). Lord Munodi's house is very beautifully and solidly constructed, but Projectors hold him in contempt for living in an old place. Projectors, for whom "progress" is everything, have little need for tradition, and even less respect for it.

The building housing the academy is another testament to their know-how. Near the building was a working mill. The projectors decided they could better it according to one of their theories, and now the mill is bone dry. The projectors, of course, blamed the man who had donated the property. Swift's message here is that the projectors are not only unfit for any useful purpose, they are blind to the fact to boot, and vindictive.

CHAPTER V

The experiments described in this chapter are based on actual experiments done or proposed by Swift's contemporaries. Included among them is an experiment designed to extract the sunbeams from cucumbers that have been hermetically sealed. During inclement summers the cucumbers are to be released to provide sunshine. Gulliver also meets an architect who has contrived a plan to build houses starting from the roof. Another man, born blind, is teaching his blind apprentices to mix colors for painters. How do they do it? They "recognize" colors by their feel and smell. Gulliver admits they frequently make mistakes.

These experiments are just plain silly. Certainly, all experiments sponsored by the Royal Society weren't so, but Swift is nonetheless making fun of the Society as a whole.

CHAPTER VI

Gulliver describes the political Projectors as appearing "wholly out of their senses," a perception that makes him "melancholy." This is Swift talking directly to you through Gulliver. He tells of schemes whereby monarchs would choose favorites on the basis of wisdom and merit, and ministers would act always with the public good uppermost in their minds. Swift is indeed discouraged by the politics of his times, for he says that his solutions for improvement are "impossible chimaeras."

Up to now Gulliver's descriptions of Projectors' activities have led us to believe that these people operate only on theories and never deal in the literal. When they do, however, the propositions are still absurd. One Projector has concluded that political bodies and natural bodies are completely analogous, and that because they are vulnerable to exactly the same maladies, ministers should be thoroughly examined after senate meetings. They would then be given proper medication, and this would solve political problems as well as physical ones. The same Projector proposed that every senator vote in opposition to his true opinion—that way, the public good would truly be served. This is Swift expressing his distrust of government officials.

The high point of this section is a Projector's suggestion for solving conflict in the senate. According to his plan, two senators with opposing opinions would be coupled; each would then have his skull sliced and they would exchange brain parts. In this way the two half-brains would debate the matter inside one skull, and this would result in a moderate senate. Surely this is folly if ever folly existed. Swift's purpose here is again to express his perception that things are desperate in English politics and that no one seems to have a reasonable idea as to what to do.

NOTE: Swift makes an acute judgment on human nature in his passage on taxation. The question under debate in Balnibarbi is whether people should be taxed for virtues or for their vices. "But, as to honour, justice, wisdom, and learning, they should not be taxed at all, because they are qualifications of so singular a kind, that no man will either allow them in his neighbour, or value them in himself." Do you agree with Swift here?

After the Projector has finished his explanation, Gulliver tells him a little about Tribnia and Langden—these are anagrams for "Britain" and "England." There, he says, the "bulk of the people consist . . . wholly of discoverers, witnesses, informers, accusers, prosecutors, evidences, swearers. . . ." Plots in government, the Projector says, are "usually the workmanship of those persons who desire . . . to restore new vigour to a crazy administration," to quell general discontent and to get rich.

NOTE: Not a pretty place, as Swift describes England, yet Gulliver says he is anxious to return there. So, as harshly as Swift has criticized his country, it would seem he does so out of concern and love for it, not out of malice. Do you think that Swift, if he unreservedly reviled Britain and honestly felt there was no hope for improvement, would exert himself writing about it, and participating in its politics?

CHAPTER VII

Gulliver leaves Lagado to explore the nearby islands. Luggnagg is his first stop. Notice Swift's saying that the island is near Japan. The mention of a real country lends reality to the imaginary Lagado. This has an effect and intention similar to Swift's use of maps, charts, and official documents.

After leaving Lagado, Gulliver goes to Glubbdubdrib, the Island of Sorcerers. The governor tells Gulliver he may summon anyone he likes from the dead.

Gulliver's initial inclination being toward "pomp and magnificence," he summons Alexander the Great, Hannibal, Caesar, Pompey, and Brutus. Who would you pick? And why? It makes sense that Swift, concerned as he is in this book with politics, would have Gulliver call up political leaders first.

Gulliver is most impressed with Brutus, who to him represents virtue, bravery, and firmness of mind. Gulliver calls up other historical figures—"destroyers of tyrants and usurpers, and the restorers of liberty to oppressed and injured nations." This is reassuring, more like the old Gulliver in Lilliput. But remember, all through Part III Gulliver is a pretty thin cover for Swift.

CHAPTER VIII

Gulliver calls up more historical figures from the dead. Homer and Aristotle head his list and are followed by commentators on these men—Didymus and Eustathius, ancient Greek writers on Homer; Duns Scotus, a proponent of Aristotle in the thirteenth century; and Petrus Ramus, a sixteenth-century French humanist who wrote criticisms of Aristotle's theories. Gulliver tells us that in the underworld the commentators kept their distance from the authors about whom they wrote out of "shame and guilt, because they had so horribly misrepresented the meaning of those authors to posterity."

NOTE: Many critics take this as Swift's opinion on literary criticism in general. Remember, part of Swift's technique is to take something very specific— Lord Munodi's house, for instance—and use it in such a way that it stands for something much larger.

Again using the example of Lord Munodi's house, think of the things it represents. A conception of beauty that is also practical, the value of tradition and gentility are just a few of the things the Lord's house stands for. What else can you come up with? In this vein, do you think it likely that Swift really intends his readers to consider the merits of the work of individual commentators? It would seem, rather, that these men are meant to represent literary commentators in general. And while we're on the subject, what do *you* think of literary commentary and criticism? In what ways has it helped your enjoyment and understanding of literary works? In what ways has it hindered? And, as you write on *Gulliver's Travels*, what will your objectives be? What do you hope to get out of it, what do you hope your readers will get out of your work?

Gulliver also calls up Descartes, whose theory that all motion is circular Swift considered bunk. Swift had some other differences with Descartes, which become clearer in Part IV. (As you begin Part IV and get acquainted with the Houhynhmns, bear in mind that Descartes thought of man as a "rational animal." Descartes valued above all else the power of rationality. Swift considered man "capable of reason," and didn't have the unmitigated reverence for reason that Descartes did.)

Returning to Glubbdubdrib, Gulliver calls up some figures who died more recently. This only confirms his disgust with modern history. Swift takes this opportunity to rail against "prostitute writers" who have greatly misled the world in the last hundred years. He also attacks politicians of the same period who achieved honors through the power of money rather than through merit. For Swift, the pinnacle of

mankind's progress was ancient Greece, and to an
even greater extent, ancient Rome.

All in all, says Swift (thinly disguised here as Gulliver), "it gave me melancholy reflections to observe
how much the race of human kind was degenerate
among us, within these hundred years past."

NOTE: We're beginning to see into the source of
the bitterness in Gulliver's letter to Richard Sympson.
Why not try to trace the development of that bitterness throughout all four parts of the *Travels*?

The low opinion of man expressed by Gulliver put
Swift in opposition to many of his contemporaries.
Swift was writing during the Enlightenment, a period
that valued progress, and considered man to be near-
ing the zenith of his intellectual and cultural powers.

CHAPTER IX

In this chapter Swift makes a wry comment on the
pomp and inhumanity that he feels often character-
izes royal rule. Gulliver is made to lick the dust before
the stool of the king of Luggnagg. Because he is a
stranger, the floor was swept before his arrival, so
Gulliver got only a small mouthful of dust. Enemies of
the king, however, receive no such amenity as a clean
floor, and often they literally choke on the dust. After
Gulliver completes this act of homage, he must say
the customary greeting: "May your Celestial Majesty
outlive the sun, eleven moons and an half." What do
you think of this greeting? Does it seem respectful, or
is it an indication that the king is a pathological ego-
tist?

CHAPTER X

In Luggnagg Gulliver meets the Struldbrugs, a group of people who are immortal. At first Gulliver is delighted at this notion, assuming that these beings enjoy perpetual youth. He finds out, however, that Struldbrugs are not forever young, they are eternally aging. They are exempt from neither illness nor senility, and at age 80 they are declared legally dead, which means that their property and wealth are passed on to the relatives who would be their heirs if they were to die. From then on the Struldbrugs live on a pittance doled out by the government. Gulliver concludes that the last thing he would ever want is to live forever.

NOTE: What do you think of immortality as lived by the Struldbrugs? What do you think Swift is telling us about his perceptions of aging and treatment of the elderly?

CHAPTER XI

Gulliver leaves Luggnagg. He has an "uneventful" trip to Japan where he catches a ship home to England.

PART IV

Part IV is the most controversial section in *Gulliver's Travels*. It is largely on the basis of Part IV that Swift has been attacked for misanthropy. There are three questions you must bear in mind as you read this book:

Is Gulliver Swift? Gulliver, as you know from the letter he wrote to his publisher, does exhibit signs of misanthropy, that is, he doesn't seem to like his fellow man very much. But might Swift have a purpose in presenting us with a misanthropic character? Might he be trying to comment on misanthropy itself? And on pride? (Remember, Swift was a cleric.) As you grapple with this question, try to imagine living in a society run by Houyhnhnms. Try to imagine living in a society run by Yahoos. Try to imagine a happy medium between these extremes, and try to imagine the society that this creature might create.

Do the Houyhnhnms represent Swift's human ideal? Think back to Descartes' theory that man is a "rational animal."

Do the Yahoos represent Swift's actual vision of mankind? If man is filled with Yahoo-like traits, is there any hope that he can improve? As you wrestle with this question you might try to balance the harsh things Gulliver has said about man in Part III, Gulliver's sometimes shameful performance in Part II, and the many forms of Lilliputian smallness in Part I, against the Christian notion that man is capable of both the best *and* the worst. Following this line of thought, man's work on earth is to come to terms with the worst he can be and try to attain the best.

Don't be discouraged. These questions have plagued critics ever since the publication of *Gulliver's Travels*. As long as you can support your viewpoint with passages from the novel, you're doing fine.

CHAPTER I

Right away Swift signals that Gulliver is in for a rough trip in Part IV. Gulliver's men suffer fevers, the survivors mutiny and put Gulliver into a long boat to make it to land if he can. Eventually, Gulliver does

make it to land. The first being he sees is a Houyhnhnm. "Upon the whole," he says, "I never beheld in
all my travels so disagreeable an animal, nor one
against which I naturally conceived so strong an
antipathy." Disgusted and confused, Gulliver strikes
the second Houyhnhnm that approaches him.

After some experience with these horses, whose
behavior is "so orderly and rational, so acute and judi-
cious," Gulliver concludes the Houyhnhnms are
magicians. For their part, they conclude that Gulliver
must be a Yahoo.

CHAPTER II

For the first time, Gulliver suspects he may be los-
ing his mind. So civilized are the Houyhnhnms they
disturb Gulliver's notions of what characteristics
apply solely to humans. When he sees that the Houyhnhnms even have servants (sorrel nags), he concludes that they "who could so far civilize brute animals, must needs excel in wisdom all the nations of
the world."

Gulliver's first meeting with a Yahoo is traumatic.
"My horror and astonishment are not to be described,
when I observed in this abominable animal a perfect
human figure. . . ." To Gulliver the Yahoos are "de-
testable on all accounts" and become "more hateful"
the more he is near them.

NOTE: What do you think of Gulliver's reaction
to the Yahoos? How do you think you would react in
Gulliver's shoes? How do you feel as you read about
the Yahoos? Attacked? Found out? Insulted? En-
raged?

Gulliver, at chapter's end, is in a sort of no-man's
land. He isn't permitted to lodge in the house with the
Houyhnhnms whom he so admires, but he isn't

made to sleep in the kennel with the Yahoos. He is neither one nor the other. Yet he makes it clear, in his last sentence, that he wishes to be counted with the horses. Would you?

CHAPTER III

From this chapter on, Gulliver does all he can to try to "become" a Houyhnhnm. He learns the language with astonishing speed—within five months he can understand everything that is said to him by the Houyhnhnms. Gulliver's host is very impressed with him, and wonders how Gulliver was taught to imitate a rational creature. In his experience, Yahoos were "the most unteachable of all brutes." Though Gulliver may be impressive to the Houyhnhnms, he still hasn't convinced them that he isn't a Yahoo.

But Gulliver presses on, determined to learn all he can about Houyhnhnms so he can take on their ways. The Houyhnhnms have no word for lying in their language, a falsehood is referred to as "the thing which was not." Gulliver is enchanted that no such vice as lying exists in this land. Indeed, this is impressive. The Houyhnhnms are equally impressed with themselves—the word Houyhnhnm means "perfection of nature."

NOTE: Do you think these creatures have named themselves aptly, or do you think the name indicates that they are self-satisfied and egotistical? At this point you probably have too little information about them to form a solid opinion, but keep the question in mind as you read on.

Gulliver continues to do his best to cover up the fact that he more nearly resembles the Yahoos than the Houyhnhnms. He never takes off his clothes, and his hosts assume his clothes constitute his skin. One night, though, Gulliver's clothes (which he used as a sort of blanket) fell off him as he slept. A servant (a sorrel nag) had been sent to tell Gulliver the master wanted to see him, and on seeing Gulliver naked takes fright that Gulliver is not the same thing night and day. The master of the house comes in to examine Gulliver, and concludes that he must be a perfect Yahoo, so smooth and fair is his body. The Houyhnhnm is mystified, however, that Gulliver should cover his body. Neither he nor his family nor any Houyhnhnm was ashamed of any part of their body, and never cover themselves. To this, Gulliver makes no reply. What would you have said? Swift here is raising the question of original sin as represented by our covering certain parts of our bodies. The Houyhnhnms have no such concept, and therefore, no such feelings of shame and guilt. Gulliver has, however; it is so ingrained in him and so disturbing to him that he can't yet bring himself to talk about it with his Houyhnhnm host.

Right after the incident with Gulliver's clothes, Gulliver begs his master not to call him a Yahoo. He repeats that he finds Yahoos "odious" and has "hatred" and "contempt" for them. And after thus presenting his case, Gulliver asks if the Houyhnhnm would keep the matter of his clothes a secret, and order the sorrel nag to do the same.

The Houyhnhnm consents to both of Gulliver's requests, as he is impressed with Gulliver's intelligence, and hopes to learn more about Gulliver and the land from which he comes. So, Gulliver's lessons resume with renewed intensity.

CHAPTER IV

By now Gulliver is fluent enough in the Houyhnhnm language to tell his master some particulars
about himself, the ways of his countrymen, and the
events of his voyage. Gulliver says he had occasion to
talk of "lying" and "false representation," both of
which his master had great difficulty understanding.
As there is no word for "lying" in the Houyhnhnm
language, there is no word for "doubt." The Houyhnhnm says that lying defeats the very purpose of language, which is to make us understand one another.
Do you think this is Swift's opinion on lying? Is it
yours? The Houyhnhnm is astonished that there are
places where Yahoos are actually in charge. Needless
to say, he's indignant that Yahoos ride on the backs of
Houyhnhnms in England, and shocked that castration of horses is a common practice. How do these
things appear to you as you try to consider them from
the viewpoint of a Houyhnhnm?

On hearing Gulliver's stories, the Houyhnhnm
decides to take a closer look at Gulliver. He judges
Gulliver's body to be very inefficient—only two feet,
eyes that cannot see very far to the side, feet so soft
they need the protection of shoes. Adding insult to
injury, he says that Gulliver lacks some of the advan-
tages of other Yahoos, long nails, for example. Gulliver's cleaner than other Yahoos this Houyhnhnm has
known, but physically, that's Gulliver's only strong
point.

NOTE: Think back to what you know about the
Enlightenment. This was a period that had an
extremely high regard for man and his achievements.
A lot of Enlightenment artwork is a tribute to what
was then considered the perfection of the human

body. The Houyhnhnms' evaluation of Gulliver's body is Swift again taking a shot at the Enlightenment.

CHAPTER V

Gulliver, at his master's request, talks in some detail about England and Europe. Gulliver describes the War of Spanish Succession and some of the differences between Catholics and Protestants. He also talks about the reasons princes wage wars: to dominate a weak neighbor; to subdue a strong one; to plunder a country that has been all but ruined by famine or a natural distaster; to take over a country in order to have its natural riches. The trade of soldier, says Gulliver, is held to be highly prestigious.

NOTE: How do you feel about what Gulliver tells his master about war? Do you feel ashamed? Do you feel shock, as the Houyhnhnm does? When Gulliver's amused at his master's reaction ("I could not forbear shaking my head and smiling a little at his ignorance"), do you share his amusement? When he again launches into a description of cannons, guns, bayonets, and the like, do you "flash back" to how you felt when Gulliver talked of gunpowder to the king of Brobdingnag? For his part, the Houyhnhnm says that "instead of reason, [Yahoos] were only possessed of some quality fitted to increase our natural vices. . . ." What do you think of this opinion? Do you think that Swift is speaking through this Houyhnhnm? Or does this sound more like the Gulliver who wrote to Richard Sympson?

At this point Gulliver's master refuses to listen to anything else about war. He has some questions about English law, specifically, how can it be, as Gulliver said, "that the law which was intended for every man's preservation, should be any man's ruin." Gulliver then explains more about the practice of law in his country. He says that lawyers are trained in proving "that white is black, and black is white." Gulliver states that lawyers hold the rest of society as virtual slaves, and are "avowed enemies to all knowledge and learning."

NOTE: Let's look closely at the lawyer incident. It accomplishes two important things. First, Swift gets to rake lawyers over the coals. Gulliver's case example makes the practice of law seem evil. Everyone damns the lawyers here—Gulliver, his master, and the reader. We are pulled in because Gulliver's tone is not judgmental, though of course his story is, but hilariously so. Too, Gulliver doesn't insist on his expertise on attorneys; in fact, he says his opinion might not be worth much as his only experience with lawyers was as their victim. This softens us—and the Houyhnhnm—to Gulliver; it makes us more receptive to the point of the story. So the second thing this accomplishes is to give Gulliver and his master something to agree on. Gulliver wins back some of the points he lost while talking of war. Do you think maybe he has a chance of really being counted a Houyhnhnm?

CHAPTER VI

Swift again uses *both* Gulliver and the Houyhnhnm to reinforce his criticisms of English life. The getting and spending of money, says Gulliver, forces people to beg, rob, steal, cheat, pimp, flatter, gamble, hector, and whore. He talks of the absurdities of importing and exporting, sending away necessities such as agricultural products and bringing in luxuries. A female Yahoo can't get her breakfast without someone having circled the world three times for the tea she drinks and the china cup she drinks it from. Considered in this light, importing and exporting do seem a little silly.

Gulliver must go to great pains to explain these things to his master, for there are no comparable words in the Houyhnhnm language for the "professional activities" mentioned above, or for disease. (Houyhnhnms feel a heaviness before they die and then peacefully pass away; there's no such thing as sickness.) Yahoos, says Gulliver, are the only animals to have imaginary diseases (by which he means hypochondriasis and psychosomatic symptoms), and doctors who deal in imaginary cures.

Gulliver next describes English politics. A head of state, says Gulliver, is "exempt from joy and grief, love and hatred, pity and anger; at least [makes] use of no other passions but a violent desire of wealth, power, and titles. . . ." He never tells the truth but with the intent that it be taken as a lie, and never lies but with the intent that he be believed. A man who wishes to become head of state can do so in one of three ways: he can marry into it; he can betray the reigning minister, and then succeed him; he can engage in a campaign to smear the courts, and so win favor for himself. Does any of this remind you of the Lilliputian court? There, too, Swift was drawing parallels to English politics. He's saying essentially the same thing here, but now he's using Gulliver as his mouthpiece. Does this necessarily mean that Gulliver is Swift?

Gulliver again makes an attempt to dissociate himself from all Yahoos. His master wishes to pay him the compliment of being a "noble Yahoo," owing to his intelligence, fair coloring, and cleanliness. At this Gulliver launches into an attack on the English nobility. He says young nobles are bred in idleness and luxury, invariably contract venereal diseases, marry only for money and position, and have children who are "rickety, or deformed."

Not only is this Swift stating his case against the English nobility, it is Gulliver stating his case against humanity as he now perceives it.

CHAPTER VII

For the first time Gulliver says straight out that he wishes never to return to a life among people. Among the Houyhnhnms, feels Gulliver, he has no example of vice, and thus the possibility of total virtuousness. How does this hit you? Are you as impressed as he is with the Houyhnhnms? As ashamed as he is to be counted among the human race?

While Gulliver was coming to this conclusion his master was also contemplating the traits characterizing Yahoos. The Houyhnhnm concedes that Yahoos had a "pittance of reason," but it served only to make them more corrupt and vice-ridden. As to Gulliver himself, the Houyhnhnm says he is inferior to other Yahoos from the point of view of physical strength, long claws, speed, etc. Yet he is like other Yahoos in that he has a deep hatred of his kind.

Yahoos hate each other more than any species on earth, says the Houyhnhnm. They fight to the death over food, treasure, tactical advantage of any kind. They destroy everything—roots, berries, fruits, animal flesh. They are gluttonous, sensation-mongers (having a likeness for a halucinogenic root that grows in the Houyhnhnms' land), disease-ridden, dirty, splenetic, and lascivious.

Reason alone, says the Houyhnhnm, is sufficient "to govern a rational creature." The Yahoo's problem is that he's short on reason.

Do you agree with the Houyhnhnm? Is rationality *all* it takes?

CHAPTER VIII

After the Houyhnhnm's description of the Yahoos in his country, Gulliver decides he needs to study them firsthand. Gulliver is given a sorrel nag as a protector as the Houyhnhnm doesn't believe that his visitor is altogether a Yahoo.

Gulliver finds baby Yahoos to be squalling, scratching imps. He also finds them smelly, with an odor resembling that of a weasel or a fox. Gulliver describes the excrement of a Yahoo baby with the same disgust he had for himself when he was in Brobdingnag. He takes care to wash thoroughly before seeing his master.

Gulliver also finds the Yahoos to be "the most unteachable of all animals," and says so in the words his master used earlier. Gulliver is trying to imitate his master.

Gulliver faces a crisis, however, when a female Yahoo is sexually attracted to him while he's swimming, and tries to attack him in the water. Needless to say, Gulliver is violently disgusted by her, but must admit that he can no longer pretend he isn't a Yahoo (animals mate naturally only within their own species).

How does Gulliver deal with this crisis? He tells us that the Yahoo who had designs on him was a good deal more attractive than the other Yahoos, and then he abruptly changes the subject, shifting attention away from himself. Clearly Gulliver is not ready, willing, or able to come to terms with the ramifications of this incident. Instead, he gives us a rundown of Houyhnhnm traits and ways. This enables him to distance himself further from the Yahoos, and lends him status, since he's once again a tour guide, telling us things we couldn't know without him. Gulliver's reaction to the crisis is to salvage his pride.

In the process we learn that the Houyhnhnms value reason beyond all else. They are *wholly* governed by it. And because there is no such thing as passion and self-interest among the Houyhnhnms, there is no such thing as dispute, doubt, opinions, argument. No "gut feelings" get in the way here. Is this reason as you know it?

The Houyhnhnms consider friendship and benevolence to be the two principal virtues. Complete strangers are treated with the decency and consideration given to close friends and relatives. Houyhnhnms don't think about romance, courtship, or love; marriages are based on efforts to strengthen the species. (A strong male will marry an attractive female, or vice versa, so that the offspring will have both traits.) Couples mate only in order to produce one offspring of each sex; after they have accomplished this they no longer have sexual relations. All marriages are arranged, yet infidelity and other marital problems don't exist. Couples live together in benevolent friendship, with feelings no more intense for each other than for anyone else they might know. If one partner is widowed before the pair has had two offspring, the survivor mates with a suitable Houyhnhnm in order to make his or her quota. And if one couple has two sons, for example, and another has two daughters, they exchange colts to even things up. The same is done with food—if a family is short, the community contributes so that everyone has the same amount to eat.

NOTE: The Houyhnhnms certainly live differently from the Yahoos here. Which Houyhnhnm ways appeal to you? Are there any so far that disturb you or turn you off? Would you, like Gulliver, wish to be a Houyhnhnm? Think about the reasons for your reactions.

CHAPTER IX

We learn more about the Houyhnhnms in this chapter, and we learn as well that Gulliver's days among them are numbered.

The most important question in the Houyhnhnm grand assembly is, Should the Yahoos be exterminated from the face of the earth? Can you imagine the U.S. Senate debating such a question? Do you think governing bodies *should* consider such a measure as a means of keeping order?

That the Yahoos are destructive, disgusting, and hateful, no one in the assembly denies. The only alternative to killing them off is proposed by Gulliver's master. After expounding on Gulliver's virtues—Gulliver, he says, is squarely between Yahoos and Houyhnhnms, as he has "a tincture" (a bit) of reason—he proposes something first described to him by Gulliver. His idea is to castrate male Yahoos. This would make them more manageable generally, and prevent them from breeding. In time the Yahoo race would just die out. (Gulliver, remember, mentioned the gelding, or castration, of horses to his Houyhnhnm master.)

NOTE: This isn't all that's going on in the grand assembly, but Gulliver's master doesn't tell him the rest in this chapter. Have you any clues as to what is being kept from Gulliver?

Gulliver tells us more about Houyhnhnm ways. They don't read or write, so all knowledge is passed on orally. Yet Gulliver says that they are very poetic, that their similes are apt, their descriptions exact, and their sentiments exalted. Their verses praise Houyhnhnm notions of friendship, benevolence, bodily strength. What do you want from poetry? Why do *you* read it, or write it? Would Houyhnhnm verse be satisfying to you?

Houyhnhnms die of old age. They don't mourn the deaths of those close to them, nor does anyone regret that he has to die. Gulliver tells the story of a Houyhnhnm who came to his master's late because she had to arrange for her husband to be buried, as he'd died that morning. During the visit she was no less cheerful than anyone else.

NOTE: What do you think of this? Philosophers, poets, artists, and scientists have long held that it is man's consciousness of his death, and his complex feelings toward it, that set him apart from other animals. Do you accept this? Does the Houyhnhnm attitude toward death and dying strike you as less than human? Does it strike you, as it apparently does Gulliver, that it is admirably rational, and something to strive for?

Where do you think Swift stands on this?

CHAPTER X

The boom is about to be lowered on Gulliver. He, however, doesn't suspect a thing. In fact, he is wholly concentrated on his happiness with the Houyhnhnms. His health is perfect, and he says he has no feelings of inconstancy toward others (except, of course, the Yahoos, whom he despises) and feels no such feelings on the part of the Houyhnhnms toward himself. He's beside himself with love and gratitude that the Houyhnhnms don't consider him a Yahoo like any other.

Nothing he learned before living with the Houyhnhnms has any value for Gulliver. When he sees his reflection in a lake or fountain he turns his face away in disgust. He could better stand the sight of a common Yahoo than himself. Why do you think this is? Because seeing himself, he recognizes that he is more Yahoo than Houyhnhnm? He takes to imitating the Houyhnhnm ways of walking, talking, gesturing. When told he "trots like a horse," he feels he's received the ultimate compliment.

But the party's over, so to speak. Gulliver's master tells him that the members of the grand assembly were offended that Gulliver, a Yahoo in spite of his abilities, was being treated like a Houyhnhnm. They gave Gulliver's host two options: 1. to put Gulliver in the kennel with the rest of the Yahoos and treat him as the rest of his kind; or 2. to make him swim back home. Because Gulliver has "some rudiments of reason," his master elects a variation on the second solution. This is not only a compliment to Gulliver, his master fears that he might use his intelligence to get revenge against the Houyhnhnms. His master has grown fond of him and doesn't wish him to drown;

he therefore proposes that Gulliver be permitted to build himself a boat.

NOTE: Were you surprised by Gulliver's getting the boot? Did you see the handwriting on the wall in Chapter IX when the assembly was contemplating annihilating all Yahoos? What do you think of their expelling Gulliver? Can you think of any instances in which he did them harm? He's guilty of one thing: he's not exactly like them. He's not exactly like anything they're familiar with, either. Gulliver falls between the categories of life (Houyhnhnms/Yahoos) as they know it.

The Houyhnhnms think of reason as a means to maintain perfectly the status quo. But the powers of reason can also be used to explore the differences between people and the ways in which they can make a society vital. It depends on what you consider to be a vital society.

Gulliver is heartbroken by this decision, yet he accepts it, vowing to spend the rest of his life praising the Houyhnhnms in the hope that it will improve his species.

On leaving the Houyhnhnms, Gulliver tries to prostrate himself in front of his master in order to kiss his hoof. You could say that Gulliver has really been brainwashed on the subject of his own inferiority. His master doesn't allow Gulliver to perform this gesture, but raises his hoof to Gulliver's mouth so that he can kiss it while standing on his feet.

NOTE: Does this strike you as a gracious gesture? (This is how it strikes Gulliver.) Or does it seem to be a touch hypocritical? After all, they've just sent poor

Gulliver packing because they don't think he's as good as they are.

CHAPTER XI

In this chapter the Gulliver who wrote the letter to Richard Sympson surfaces. On his way home Gulliver is rescued by a Portuguese ship. Hearing human talk for the first time in a long while, Gulliver describes it as "monstrous." Gulliver has obviously been deeply traumatized by his stay with the Houyhnhnms, and his conduct is as much Houyhnhnm as human. The captain of the ship, Pedro de Mendez, is exceedingly gentle and kind to Gulliver, and even pays his way from Lisbon to England. Yet Gulliver says he had to try hard to "conceal [his] antipathy to human kind, although it often broke out." Even this the captain pretended to not notice.

When he sees his family Gulliver is filled with "hatred, disgust, and contempt." He is horrified that he's ever had sexual relations with these Yahoos. As soon as his wife embraces him (he's been gone five years) he faints, overcome with revulsion.

He can't abide the smell or sight of his wife and children, refuses to eat in the same room with them, and won't allow them to touch him or his food. He immediately buys some horses, and spends most of his time in the stable "conversing" with them.

NOTE: Clearly Gulliver is mad. Do you think it's because he had a glimpse of perfection (as represented by the Houyhnhnms) and realized he could never attain it? Or is it that he hasn't been able to come to terms with what it means to be human, that he is "only human"?

CHAPTER XII

Gulliver makes a point of stressing the truth in all that he has recounted of his voyages. In so doing he compares himself to Sinon, an ancient Roman famous for being a liar. Remember that Swift has throughout this book given "proof" of incidents and places. Here he's calling attention to the fact that this work is fictional. This presents us with a conflict (and an excellent point to raise if you're arguing that Gulliver is *not* Swift): Gulliver's work, to his twisted mind, is true; yet Swift's is fiction.

Gulliver says that he writes for "the noblest end, to inform and instruct mankind. . . . " He's fit for the task because his exposure to the Houyhnhnms has rendered him "superior" to his fellows.

He's trying to readjust to life among his Yahoo family. He now allows his wife to eat with him, though he still keeps his nostrils stuffed with lavender or tobacco so as not to be bothered by the smell. He even forces himself to look in a mirror every day to get used to his human face and those of the people around him.

Gulliver ends with an exhortation against pride. How ironic, for Gulliver has proved himself exceedingly proud.

This is a particularly brilliant device. Swift uses Gulliver to express his feelings about the sinfulness of pride, yet Gulliver can't live up to Swift's exhortation.

Gulliver isn't the only one to have had a long journey. So have we.

A STEP BEYOND

Tests and Answers

TESTS

Test 1

1. *Gulliver's Travels* was intended as _____
   A. a glorification of eighteenth-century England
   B. A comdemnation of certain human traits
   C. escapist literature

2. Sizes and measurements in Lilliput become normal if we multiply everything by _____
   A. four   B. six   C. twelve

3. Gulliver finds the Lilliputians _____
   A. proud and corrupt
   B. ingenious and forgiving
   C. suspicious but fun-loving

4. Gulliver falls into disfavor with the Emperor _____
   A. because of the way he put out the palace fire
   B. when he refuses to help him enslave Blefuscu
   C. when a rumor spreads of a scandal involving Gulliver and the wife of a high official

5. Gulliver's friend among the Lilliputian officials is _____
   A. Bolgolam   B. Flimnap   C. Reldresal

6. Which statement is true?   _____
   A. the King of Blefuscu turns out to be kinder
      than the Emperor of Lilliput
   B. after returning to England, Gulliver made a
      fortune in exhibiting one of the little people
      he had hidden in his pocket
   C. important positions in Lilliput were given
      out according to an individual's height.

7. The Prince of Lilliput walked with a hobble   _____
   because
   A. he was born lame
   B. he was wounded in the battle with the
      Blefuscudians
   C. the heels of one of his shoes was slightly
      higher than the other

8. Gulliver finds the size of the Brobdingnagians _____
   A. magnifies their physical blemishes to the
      point of disgust
   B. helps him appreciate the beauty of his
      English countrymen
   C. arouses a feeling of envy within him

9. Which is true?   _____
   A. Gulliver is almost killed by a hazelnut
      thrown at him during his performance
   B. Gulliver's performance at the Green Eagle
      Inn consists of singing and dancing
   C. The farmer is very careful not to exhaust
      Gulliver with too many performances as it
      might ruin a very profitable business

10. After listening to Gulliver's account of life in _____
    England, the King
    A. mildly reprimands him for inventing this
       "fiction"
    B. pronounces his sympathies are with the
       Whigs

   C. expresses an opinion about the Whigs and
     Tories which is similar to Gulliver's
     opinion about the Big-Endians and Little-
     Endians

11. Swift has been called one of the greatest satirists in the
    English language. Describe Swiftian satire.

12. On the basis of *Gulliver's Travels*, discuss Swift's notions
    of a good and just government.

13. Find support in the *Travels* for the statement, "Human
    nature is petty."

14. Find support in the *Travels* for the statement, "Human
    nature is magnanimous and just."

15. Discuss the limits of reason as found in *Gulliver's Trav-
    els*.

Test 2

1. Gulliver is forced to defend himself against   _____
   A. the royal dwarf
   B. the flies and wasps
   C. the beggars of Brobdingnag

2. The episode with the Queen's maids of   _____
   honor
   A. reflects the moral behavior of English court
     ladies
   B. shows Swift's avoidance of gross physical
     details
   C. shows that palace intrigues do not depend
     on the size of the participants

3. Gulliver leaves the land of the giants when   _____
   the
   A. Kings orders his expulsion
   B. nurse reluctantly helps him build a boat
   C. box he was left in is carried away by an
     eagle

4. Which is not true of the scientists of Laputa? _____
   A. they need servants to remind them they
      are in the middle of a conversation
   B. their wives deceive them at every
      opportunity
   C. their experiments are aimed at improving
      the standard of living

5. Which is an undertaking of the Academy of _____
   Projectors?
   A. extracting sunbeams from cucumbers
   B. transmuting lead into gold
   C. growing wool on animals other than
      sheep

6. The Sturldbruggs are _____
   A. happy because they live forever
   B. miserable because they lose their youth
      and health at the same age as mortals
   C. the teachers and purveyors of wisdom
      because of their unlimited experience

7. The Houyhnhnms at first do not regard _____
   Gulliver as a Yahoo because of his
   A. clothing
   B. speech
   C. ability to survive on his own

8. Gulliver explains to the Houyhnhnms that the _____
   rulers in his land govern
   A. by virtue of their power of reasoning far
      beyond that of the brutish Yahoos
   B. an intricate system of succession and
      parliamentary rules
   C. by circumventing their physical ineffi-
      ciency with weapons

9. The most despicable characteristic of the _____
   Yahoos is
   A. pride   B. greed   C. ambition

10. The visit to the country of the Houyhnhnms _____
    A. leaves Gulliver insane
    B. proves the possibility of "educating" the animal world
    C. convinces Gulliver that there is no real difference between men and beasts

11. Discuss the ways in which Swift plays with notions of "big" and "small" in *Gulliver's Travels*.

12. Discuss Swift's handling of pride in the *Travels*.

13. What is the function of religion in *Gulliver's Travels*?

14. Discuss Swift and his relationship to the Enlightenment.

15. Why is *Gulliver's Travels* relevant today?

ANSWERS

Test 1

1. B   2. B   3. A   4. B   5. C   6. A
7. C   8. A   9. A   10. C

   11.   Think in terms of two things: the objects of Swift's satire, and the techniques that go into Swift's satire.

   Think back over the novel. In Part I, for example, Swift satirizes the court of George I. His primary satirical device here is allegory—the Lilliputian government leaders stand for Whig leaders in the tumultuous years between 1708 and 1726. In Part II it is Gulliver who represents English attitudes Swift wishes to criticize. In Part III the Projectors are allegories for certain members of the Royal Society, whom Swift was attacking satirically. In Part IV the allegories are not so clear-cut; the Yahoos and the Houyhnhnms are both exaggerated representations. Just as the Houyhnhnms aren't intended to represent Swift's human ideal, neither do the Yahoos represent his opinion of mankind. It is Gulliver, because he can't see Swift's distinction, who is the brunt of Swift's satire.

Go through the book carefully, taking special note of the ways in which Swift uses allegory, irony, and shifts in perspective to launch his attacks.

12. Compare the Lilliputian emperor with the Brobdingnagian king. Also, consider the role of government in the funding of scientific and academic research. Think in terms of Part III as you reflect on the second part of this question.

13. Start by examining the attitudes and practices of the Lilliputians, the many ways in which they are small. Then take a close at look at Gulliver and the ways in which he's Lilliputian compared to the king of Brobdingnag. Don't forget to reflect on the Laputans and Projectors and the extent to which they allow themselves to be cut off from the world because of their individual abstract preoccupations.

14. Think about Gulliver and the restraint, patience, and faithfulness to justice he shows in Part I. Consider the king of Brobdingnag, the kindness he and his wife show Gulliver, and the ways in which he governs his country. Think, too, of the courtesy he shows Gulliver even after Gulliver tells him about gunpowder. As you're answering this question break down the Houyhnhnm composite. Owing to their great stores of reason, the Houyhnhnms have eradicated vices such as lying, corruption, infidelity, etc., from their society. In certain ways their society does reflect the best we're capable of—enduring peace, for one. Don't forget Captain Pedro de Mendez, who is exceedingly kind to Gulliver at the end of Part IV.

15. In answering Question 14 you thought about the admirable aspects of a society governed entirely by reason. Now think about the aspects of life among the Houyhnhnms that are less attractive, less desirable, less *human*. For example, there is no feeling of kinship among the Houyhnhnms. Neither is there any such thing as falling in love. The personal joys connected with conceiving a baby, giving birth, and raising a family are nonexistent. Even life itself seems less precious—no one minds dying, and no one mourns the death of anyone else.

Test 2

1. B   **2.** A   **3.** C   **4.** C   **5.** A   **6.** B
7. A   **8.** C   **9.** B   **10.** A

11.   Consider Gulliver when he appeared very big in the land of Lilliput. In many ways he was grotesque. Yet finally it was the Lilliputians, fine and small though they are, who proved to truly be grotesque. Think now of the Brobdingnagians. Physically they are repulsive to Gulliver, as grotesque as he was in Lilliput. Yet it is the giants compared to Gulliver who are refined.

Swift accomplishes two things here. The Lilliputians are literally small; they are also figuratively small (small-minded and narrow of spirit). To the eye they're attractive, yet to the mind's eye they're not. The Brobdingnagians are literally and figuratively big (large in their sympathies, big-hearted, open-minded). To the eye they're not pleasant to look at, yet how they please the mind's eye!

Think as well of the ways in which Gulliver when he feels (and is) so small, tries to make himself bigger. To cite the most obvious example, he tries to impress the king with the powers of gunpowder. Consider, too, how awful it is for Gulliver to be small, how shameful he begins to feel, how violent and disgusted and vengeful.

12.   This question is linked to Question 11, dealing with notions of "big" and "little."

Think about the tiny Lilliputians and their grandiose ceremonies, their imposing bureaucracy, and the craftiness with which they exact their revenge. Think, too, about Gulliver in Part II, and the repeated attacks to his self-image and feelings of security—he's often injured, made fun of by the dwarf, hired out as a freak, loved more as a puppy than a man, etc. In answering this question deal with both the evidences of pride and the factors that lessen our vulnerability to the sin of pride.

Keep in mind that in Part IV Gulliver is lost because he's totally isolated. He's neither a Yahoo nor a Houyhnhnm; in other words, he retreats from being human, part animal/part man. The Yahoos, you remember, are savage at least partly because they're cut off from their Yahoo society.

13. Religion has various functions in this novel. In Lilliput it is a means to attain power and an excuse by which to dominate—even enslave—others. Since you know that the Lilliputians stand for the Whigs, Swift's enemies, you can deduce Swift's opinion on religion as handled by the Lilliputians.

In Part III, where tradition has no place, religion has no value. The closest they come here is astrology, if you consider religion to be primarily mystical. If you consider religion as a constant, guiding force in a person's life, then in Part III abstract science constitutes religion.

The Houyhnhnms have no need of religion. There is nothing they question, nothing that awes them, nothing that frightens them. Swift evidently finds this an impossibly sterile way to be alive.

It's important to consider that Gulliver is lost because he doesn't understand what Swift thinks is the function of religion. For Swift, religion helps man to improve himself spiritually while he is on earth. Gulliver misunderstands Swift's presenting him with the Yahoos. Gulliver thinks that people are Yahoos; Swift's message is that Yahoos are what we must strive to not become.

14. You know already that the Enlightenment was an age that exalted the powers of reason, that believed that man was essentially good (and therefore needful of the redemption prescribed by traditional religion), that valued above all else that which was new. The Enlightenment was the beginning of the modern age.

Think of Swift and his satire in Part III against the Royal Society. Think, too, of his sympathetic Count Munodi. Examine carefully the limits of reason as they appear in Part IV.

15.   For starters, Swift is dealing with human nature, the abiding weaknesses and strengths of people. We certainly haven't solved the problems of government, so Swift's work is far from dated on that score.

Just as Swift was on the brink of the modern age, we are new to the nuclear age. Gunpowder was the worst weapon on earth during Swift's lifetime; today we have nuclear bombs. What do you think Swift would have thought of the A-bomb? What do you think he'd have thought of our government subsidizing billions of dollars of research into nuclear arms? And of many of our brightest young scientists seeking to be involved in this research?

Term Paper Ideas

1. Identify the various targets of Swift's satire in the *Travels*.

2. How does allegory serve Swift in the making of his satire?

3. How does irony serve Swift in the making of his satire?

4. How does the character of Gulliver serve Swift in the making of his satire?

5. Discuss the ways in which Swift manipulates point of view so that the reader at times becomes the target of Swift's satire.

6. Discuss the ways in which Swift gets the reader to accept the fantastical people, places, and phenomena in the *Travels*.

7. Discuss Swift's concept of man.

8. Which aspects of human nature does Swift find admirable?

9. Which aspects of human nature does Swift find lamentable?

10. To which sin does Swift consider man most vulnerable?

11. What is Swift's overall opinion of man?

12. Discuss Swift's opinion on the values of reason.

13. Discuss Swift's opinion on the limits of reason.

14. Discuss Swift's ideas on the value of tradition.

15. What criteria do you think Swift would enforce if he were in charge of evaluating government grants for scientific and academic research?

16. Compare and contrast Descartes' notion of man as a *rational animal* and Swift's notion of man as an *animal capable of reason*.

17. Compare and contrast the aims of the typical travel book written in Swift's time, and the aims of *Gulliver's Travels*. Examine the elements of eighteenth-century travel books that Swift satirizes in *Gulliver's Travels*.

18. Discuss the Yahoos as a symbol of man.

19. Discuss the ways in which Swift ensures that you will believe and side with Gulliver when he wants you to.

20. Discuss the ways in which Swift ensures that you'll be suspicious of Gulliver, be on your guard against him, and be critical of him.

Further Reading

CRITICAL WORKS

Books

Ehrenpreis, Irvin. *Swift: The Man, His Works, and the Age.* Cambridge: Cambridge University Press, 1962. The definitive modern biography.

Quintana, Ricardo. *The Mind and Art of Jonathan Swift.* Magnolia, MA: Peter Smith, 1953. A superb overall introduction.

Williams, Kathleen. *Jonathan Swift and the Age of Compromise.* 1958.

Articles

Carnochan, W. B. "Gulliver: The Satirist on Himself," in *Lemuel Gulliver's Mirror for Man.* Berkeley: University of California Press, 1968. An excellent article on the ways in which Swift uses Gulliver in order to satirize himself.

Crane, R. S. "The Houyhnhnms, the Yahoos, and the History of Ideas," in *Reason and the Imagination,* ed. J. A. Mazzeo. New York: Columbia University Press, 1962, pp. 243–53. This article deals with the question of Swift's thoughts on what it is to be human.

Dyson, A. E. "Swift: The Metamorphosis of Irony," in *Essays and Studies.* London: The English Association, 1958, pp. 53–67. A fine discussion of Swift's satirical techniques; especially strong on Part IV.

Elliott, Robert C. "The Satirist Satirized," in *The Power of Satire.* Princeton: Princeton University Press, 1960, pp. 184–214.

Landa, Louis A. "Jonathan Swift," in *English Institute Essays.* New York: Columbia University Press, 1946, pp. 20-35. Fascinating discussion of the history of reaction to the *Travels.*

Lawlor, John. "The Evolution of Gulliver's Character," in *Essays and Studies*. London: The English Association, 1955, pp. 69–73.

Monk, Samuel Holt. "The Pride of Lemuel Gulliver." *The Sewanee Review*, 63 (1955): 48–71.

Voigt, Milton. "The Sources of Gulliver's Travels," in *Swift and the Twentieth Century*. Detroit: Wayne State University Press, 1964, pp. 65–76.

Wedel, T. O. "On the Philosophical Background of *Gulliver's Travels*." *Studies in Philology*, 23 (1926): 434–50. Very helpful, especially with regard to Part IV.

AUTHOR'S OTHER WORKS

A Tale of a Tub and *The Battle of the Books*, 1704. Satires on religious and academic corruption.

The Journal to Stella. Letters written to Esther Johnson 1710–14; published in 1766.

A Modest Proposal, 1713. Scathing satire against the English for their attempts to "colonize" Ireland. Considered by many to be the finest satire ever written in English.

Drapier's Letters, 1724. Swift's public, though pseudonymous, letters protesting the introduction of a debased coinage into Ireland. Three hundred pounds was offered for the identification of the author, but Swift was never turned in though everyone in Ireland knew he was the author. The debased currency was not introduced because of Swift's satirical outcry.

Verses on the Death of Dr. Swift, 1730.

The Legion Club 1736.

Glossary

Allegory A story in which characters, situations, and places have a significance beyond what they are themselves; characters, situations, and places that represent something or someone else; the aim of allegory is to teach or edify.

Balnibarbi An island ruled by the king of Laputa. Found in Part III.

Blefuscu Lilliput's enemy. Blefuscu is an allegorical representation of France. Occurs in Part I.

Bolingbroke, Henry St. John (1678–1751) Tory leader.

Brobdingnag Land of the giants visited by Gulliver in Part II.

Brobdingnagians Inhabitants of Brobdingnag.

George I Hanoverian king of England 1714–27; favored the Whigs. Satirized by Swift in Part I, allegorized by the Lilliputian emperor.

Glubdubdrib Island of Sorcerers visited by Gulliver in Part III.

Houyhnhnms Totally rational horses idealized by Gulliver in Part IV.

Irony A device in which the meaning of a statement or action is opposite to that which is presented.

Laputa Flying island encountered by Gulliver in Part III. It is inhabited by foolish, wildly impractical visionaries.

Lilliput Land visited by Gulliver in Part I; its inhabitants are six inches high.

Lilliputians Inhabitants of the land of Lilliput.

Lindalino City that rebelled against Laputa; allegory for Dublin rebelling against England.

Luggnagg Island Gulliver visits in Part III, home of the Struldbruggs, who are immortal.

Misanthrope One who hates and/or avoids other people. Swift was accused of misanthropy; Gulliver actually is a misanthrope by the novel's end.

Nardac Title of honor bestowed by the Lilliputian emperor on Gulliver after he seizes the Blefuscudian Fleet.

Oxford, Earl of Robert Harley, Tory leader eventually ousted by Bolingbroke in 1714.

Queen Anne English queen 1702–14; last of the Stuart monarchs, favored the Tories.

Satire A mocking attack against vices, stupidities, follies, with an aim to educate or edify.

Struldbruggs A race of immortals who live in Luggnagg, found in Part III.

Tories One of two rival political parties in England. The Tories tended in Swift's time to support more wholeheartedly the Church of England, to support the monarchy in favor of the newer, merchant classes, and to be generally more conservative than the Whigs. Swift was a Tory from 1710 on.

Walpole, Sir Robert (1676–1745) Whig prime minister 1715–17 and 1721–42. Swift's enemy.

Whigs One of two rival political parties in England. During Swift's time the Whigs tended to support the newer, merchant classes in favor of the monarchy and the gentry, were more in step with the Enlightenment, and were generally more liberal than the Tories.

Yahoos Odious humanoids Swift uses to allegorize the worst traits to be found in human nature.

The Critics

I congratulate you first upon what you call your Couzen's wonderful Book, which is *publica trita manu* at present, and I prophecy will be in future the admiration of all men. . . .

I find no considerable man very angry at the book; some indeed think it rather too bold, and too general a Satire: but none that I hear of accuse it of particular reflections (I mean no persons of consequence, or good judgment; the mob of Criticks, you know, always are desirous to apply Satire to those that they envy for being above them). . . . Motte receiv'd the copy (he tells me) he knew not from whence, nor from whom, dropp'd at his house in the dark, from a Hackney-coach: by computing the time, I found it was after you left England, so for my part, I suspend my judgment.

—*Alexander Pope to Swift, November 16, 1726*

I wondered to hear him say of *Gulliver's Travels*, "When once you have thought of big men and little men, it is very easy to do all the rest." I endeavoured to make a stand for Swift, and tried to rouse those who were much more able to defend him. . . ."

—*Boswell*, Life of Johnson, 1775

Swift's greatness lies in the intensity, the almost insane violence, of that "hatred of bowels" which is the essence of his misanthropy and which underlies the whole of this book.

—*Aldous Huxley*, Do What You Will, 1930

Animal rationale-animal rationis capax! Swift's somewhat scholastic distinction turns out, in the light of seventeenth century thought, to be by no means scholastic. It symbolizes, in fact, the chief intellectual battle of the age. Swift seems to have seen clearly enough that in assaulting man's pride in reason, he was attacking the new optimism at its very root.

> —*T.O. Wedel, "On the Philosophical Background of* Gulliver's Travels," *from* Studies in Philology, 23 (1926).

I tell you after all that I do not hate Mankind, it is *vous autres* who hate them because you would have them reasonable Animals, and are Angry for being disappointed. I have always rejected that definition and made another of my own.

> —*Jonathan Swift to Alexander Pope, November 26, 1725*